Are you religious? Do you sometimes feel you have been trapped into playing a game called "church"?

This book shows why "religion" has failed and points to the way to be a Christian without being "religious."

HOW TO BE A CHRISTIAN WITHOUT BEING RELIGIOUS

The Book of Romans in **Living Letters** paraphrase
combined with illustrated contemporary comment

EDITED BY FRITZ RIDENOUR

A Division of G/L Publications
Glendale, California, U.S.A.

A teaching and discussion guide for use with this book is available from your church supplier.

Over 1,200,000 in print

Second Printing, 1967
Third Printing, 1967
Fourth Printing, 1968
Fifth Printing, 1968
Sixth Printing, 1968
Seventh Printing, 1968
Eighth Printing, 1969
Ninth Printing, 1969
Tenth Printing, 1969
Eleventh Printing, 1970
Twelfth Printing, 1970
Thirteenth Printing, 1971

Published by
Regal Book Division, G/L Publications
Glendale, California 91209, U.S.A.

FOREWORD

This book is a team effort.

It began when Paul, the great apostle, penned his famous epistle to the church at Rome around A.D. 57.

Next came Ken Taylor's *Living Letters*, the paraphrased epistles. Taylor's paraphrase, in simple English, of the New Testament letters first appeared in 1962. It became an immediate favorite, with 1,750,000 copies printed in its first five years. Our special thanks goes to Mr. Taylor and Tyndale House Publishers for allowing us to make the *Living Letters* paraphrase of Romans the backbone of this book.

Our thanks, too, to freelance writer Henk Vigeveno who contributed material for several of the chapters, particularly 1, 2, and 8.

Finally, my personal thanks to the members of the Gospel Light editorial team that added contemporary comment and cartoons to help catch the spirit of Biblical Christianity:

Joyce Thimsen, Art Director of Gospel Light Publications, did the cartoons.

Georgiana Walker, Assistant Youth Editor and Dian Ritzenthaler, editorial assistant, covered the multitude of details involved in manuscript checking, proofreading, retyping.

The final result is, we hope, a handbook on how to be a Christian without the burdens of being religious, a book that helps you see the power and potential in Jesus Christ, so that you can "confidently and joyfully look forward to becoming all that God has in mind for you to be."

Fritz Ridenour
Youth Editor, Gospel Light Publications

Shouldn't a Christian "Be Religious"?

How to Be a Christian Without Being Religious almost sounds like a contradiction in terms. Christianity is called one of the world's great religions, is it not?

According to Webster, a religion is a system of faith and of worship ...

Christianity is certainly that.

According to Webster, a religion is the service to and adoration of God expressed in forms of worship ...

Christianity is certainly that, too.

According to Webster, religion is devotion, fidelity, conscientiousness, an awareness or conviction of the existence of a supreme being, which arouses reverence, love, gratitude, the will to obey and serve ...

Christianity is certainly that ... and more.

It is the "more" that is behind the title of this book.

Christianity is more than a religion, because every religion has one basic characteristic. Its followers are trying to reach God, find God, please God through their own efforts. Religions reach up toward God. Christianity is God reaching down to man. Christianity claims that men have not found God, but *that God has found them.* To some this is a crushing blow. They prefer religious effort—dealing with God on their own terms. This puts them in control. They feel good about "being religious."

Christianity, however, is not religious striving.

To practice Christianity is to *respond* to what God has done for you. The Christian life is a relationship with God, not a religious treadmill. Many Christians, however, behave like they really don't believe this. With form, formalism, ritual, legalism, rules, systems and formulas we attempt to reduce Christianity to a religion—a system of some kind where works are really substituted for faith and trust, where law takes precedence over grace. We will not necessarily admit this, but it's true nonetheless. Instead of responding to God's love, we reach out for it—and neatly keep God at arm's length while we do so.

But God will not stay at arm's length. When He comes into your life He demands all of it. Away with religious pretense and pontificating. Away with your religious game called "church" that you play so well every Sunday. God wants *all* of you—

THIS BOOK DEFINES
"BEING RELIGIOUS"
AS TRYING TO . . .

. . . REACH GOD

. . . FIND GOD.

. . . PLEASE GOD

. . . THROUGH YOUR OWN FUTILE EFFORTS.

ALTHOUGH THEY MAY NOT REALIZE IT, MANY CHRISTIANS LIVE ON A RELIGIOUS TREADMILL...

...AND THE RESULT IS FRUSTRATION, A FREQUENT SENSE OF FAILURE.

your heart, your soul, your body—as a living sacrifice to Him.

Is there a way to be a Christian without being religious? Is there some kind of surgical tool that will help us cut through the façade that leaves many of us feeling deep within that "Christianity is really 'being good' and if I'm not good, I haven't made the grade, and if I haven't made the grade I'm left feeling frustrated, guilty, and really not very happy with myself or my faith."

Yes, there is such a tool. It is a single book of the New Testament—Paul's letter to the Romans. In 16 brief chapters the great apostle shows you that Christianity is far more than a religion. He tells you who you really are, why you are living, how to get the most out of life. In short, in the following chapters you can find out for yourself about how to be a Christian without being religious.

CHAPTER 1

Your faith...

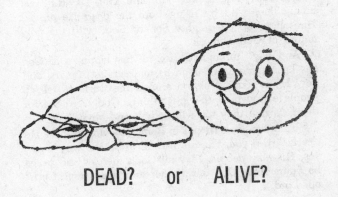

DEAD?   or   ALIVE?

An odd question . . . or is it? Let's define terms. A person's faith is what he believes, the guiding principles and hope for his life. "Dead faith" is the kind that rests on little more than an intellectual system, dry and dusty credos, meaningless dogmas that have little to do with life as it really is. A "live faith" is just the opposite. To have a living faith means more than mental assent to a statement of beliefs. A living faith puts you in touch with God. A living faith has power. Paul opens his letter to Rome on this note . . .

1

Dear Friends in Rome,

¹This letter is from Paul, Jesus Christ's slave, chosen to be a missionary, and sent out to preach God's Good News.

²This Good News was promised long ago by God's prophets in the Old Testament; ³it is the Good News about His Son, Jesus Christ our Lord, Who came as a human baby, for He was born into King David's royal family line; ⁴and by rising from the dead He proved Himself to be the mighty Son of God, with the holy nature of God Himself.

⁵And now, through Christ, all the kindness of God has been poured out upon us undeserving sinners, and now He is sending us out around the world to tell all people everywhere the great things God has done for them, so that they too will believe and obey Him.

⁶⁻⁷And you, dear friends in Rome, are among those He dearly loves; you, too, are invited to be His very own—yes, His holy people. May all God's mercies and peace be yours from God our Father and from Jesus Christ our Lord.

⁸Let me say first of all that wherever I go I hear you being talked about! For your faith in God is becoming known around the world. How I thank God through Jesus Christ for this good report, and for each one of you. ⁹God knows how often I pray for you. Day and night I bring you and your needs in prayer to the One I serve with all my might, telling others the Good News about His Son.

¹⁰And one of the things I keep on praying for is the opportunity, God willing, to come at last to see you and if possible that I will have a safe trip. ¹¹For I long to see you so that I can bring you some spiritual food that will help you grow strong in the Lord. ¹²Then, too, I

need your help, for I not only want to share my faith with you but be encouraged by yours. In that way each of us will be a blessing to the other.

13I want you to know, dear brothers, that I planned to come many times before (but God did not let me) to work among you and see good results, as I have among the other Gentile churches. 14For I owe a great debt to you and to everyone else, both to civilized peoples and heathen nations; yes, to the educated and uneducated alike. 15So, to the fullest extent of my ability, I am ready to come to you in Rome also to preach God's Good News.

16For I am not ashamed of this Good News about Christ. It is God's powerful method of bringing all who believe it to heaven. This message was preached first to the Jews alone, but now everyone is invited to come to God in this same way.

17This Good News tells us that God makes us ready for heaven—good in His eyes—when we put our faith and trust in Christ to save us. And the more we trust Him the more clearly we can see* that He has taken away our sins and filled us with His goodness. As the Old Testament says it, the man who finds life will find it through trusting God.

Must a Christian "assassinate his brains"?

The opening paragraphs of Romans are strange words for a man who once hated Christianity. Paul was a Jew. He became a rabbi and belonged to the religious conservatives of his time, the Pharisees. Immediately following Christ's death and resurrec-

*literally: "(this) righteousness of God is *revealed* from faith to faith," i.e., we see ever more clearly what God has done for us, step by step, as our faith grows stronger.

tion in A.D. 33, Paul tried desperately to exterminate Christianity. Paul *knew* the Christians were wrong. They claimed that Jesus was the promised Messiah, the Saviour—utter nonsense!

But on one of his campaigns to persecute Christians (see Acts, chapter 9) Paul was struck to the ground by a blinding vision. He heard the voice of the living Christ, and he was changed. Paul did a complete about face. He left the Pharisees (at the peril of his life) and became a devoted Christian, "a bondslave" of Christ. And from the start Paul knew that being a Christian was not a matter of being "religious." He had had plenty of religion as a Pharisee. He knew the law like you know the alphabet. Still, the law did not bring him peace. It did not put him in touch with the living God. But on that dusty road to Damascus, Paul got the message. God reached down to him and asked, "Why persecutest thou Me?" and Paul responded by saying, "Lord, what wilt thou have me to do?"

Paul became an acknowledged leader of the early Church. He established groups of believers everywhere and wrote many letters to encourage them in their new faith. The epistle to the Romans is the only letter he wrote to a place he had not yet visited. Paul was anxious to reach Rome. He hoped to make the capital city of the Roman Empire a jumping off place for more missionary work to the west—possibly Spain. While staying with friends in Corinth, Paul wrote to the church at Rome to give the members a better understanding of the meaning of the gospel. And in these opening lines

4

THE GOSPEL IS NOT MAN-MADE IDEAS

Paul wastes no time in getting around to why Christianity is a living faith.

"For I am not ashamed of the gospel of Christ: for it is the power of God unto salvation to everyone that believeth; to the Jew first, and also to the Greek" (Rom. 1:16).

Paul was ready to share the gospel—the Good News—because he knew that here was power. The gospel gives meaning to life. It can deliver the goods. In Paul's day, men constantly sought salvation—peace of mind and heart, peace for their souls. Men still seek salvation today, but somehow they miss the real message of the gospel. In far too many circles Christianity has been reduced to another religion, complete with rituals, rules and all necessary accouterments to "reach up to God." But this is not the gospel. There are several things the gospel *is not*:

The gospel is not laws and burdens. It is not a religious list of "you can't do this . . . you can't do that . . . hands off . . . mustn't touch . . . do this or die."

Nor is the gospel man-made ideas. Many people have a God, but they keep him small—small enough to fit in the religious "box" they call their brand of Christianity.

And the gospel is not anti-intellectual, another claim made by some who prefer a sophisticated religion that is "worthy of one's intelligence." You don't have to assassinate your brains to be a Christian, as many outstanding men can testify. Lambert Dolphin, Jr., research physicist at Stanford University, says: "I wasn't even a true scientist

6

THE GOSPEL IS
GOOD NEWS FROM GOD

until I met Jesus Christ. I couldn't be for I was cut off from reality. Life with God is the only reality. And that is possible only through faith in Jesus Christ and His atoning death for our sins. Jesus Christ is the answer to the secret of the universe. In Him I've found the reason for life and the key to everything."*

J. Edgar Hoover, famed director of the FBI, has said: "There is respect for human dignity only where Christ and the Bible are a way of life."†

Walter F. Burke, general manager of Project Mercury and Gemini, says: "I have found nothing in science or space exploration to compel me to throw away my Bible or to reject my Saviour, Jesus Christ, in whom I trust."‡

The gospel is good news from God in Jesus Christ.

---

*From *Today*, Oct. 16, 1966. Copyright 1966. Harvest Publications.
†From *Trust in the Lord* by Jean Ehly. Syndicated article, Singer Features.
‡From *Ten Scientists and What They Believe.* Copyright 1963. David C. Cook Publishing Company.

Through Christ, God the Creator, involved Himself with man, His creation. In the gospel, God is saying to man, "I love you; the burden is off your back. I have reached down to do something for you. Christ died for your sin, your guilt, your inadequacy. And Christ rose again. He lives and if your personal faith is in Him, you live also . . ."

One more point from Paul's opening remarks: *The gospel is for undeserving sinners.* (See Rom. 1:5.) That's what makes it such good news. It's for those who know they can't reach up to God on their religious own, for those who are even a little bit desperate. The gospel is not religion. The gospel is Christianity—faith in and commitment to a Person—Jesus Christ. And that, as we shall see, is what Romans is all about . . .

For further thought

1. Take a sheet of paper and write your definition of "the gospel." What does the Good News mean to you personally? Can you list three to six ways the gospel affects your life?

2. Memorize Rom. 1:16. Then do a study of the word "salvation" by summarizing the following Bible verses: Ps. 37:39; Acts 4:12; Heb. 2:10, 5:9; Gal. 1:4; Eph. 2:9; II Tim. 1:9; Titus 3:5.

3. Do you agree or disagree with this statement by Martin Luther (leader of the Protestant Reformation)? "Whatever your heart clings to and relies on is your God." Write down some reasons for your answer.

CHAPTER 2

Does God ever grade on the curve?

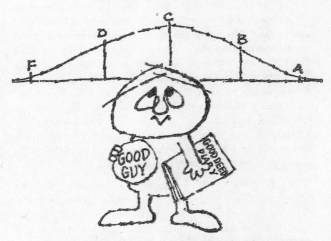

"Grading on the curve" is a familiar term to the high school or college student. The teacher takes all the scores and lists them from highest to lowest. Then he plots a "curve" that finds some students falling in the A category, others in B, many in the C range, and the lower scores fall into D and F positions. Does God grade men this way? A lot of people talk like they think so: "Well, I'm not half as bad as . . . I live a pretty good life. I never steal, or cheat . . . Why I don't even kick my dog . . ." Surely God, in His benevolent love and kindness, will give a passing grade and heavenly diploma to people who "do their best"? Let us see what Paul says . . .

18But God shows His anger from heaven against all sinful, evil men who push away the truth. 19For the truth about God is known to them by instinct; God has put this knowledge in their hearts. 20Since earliest times men have seen the earth and sky and all God made, and have known of His existence and great eternal power. So they have no excuse for saying they don't know whether or not there is a God. 21Yes, they knew about Him all right, but they wouldn't admit it or worship Him or even thank Him for all His daily care. And after a while they began to think up silly ideas of what God was like and what He wanted them to do. The result was that their foolish minds became dark and confused. 22Claiming themselves to be wise without God, they became utter fools instead.

23And then, instead of worshiping the glorious ever-living God, they took wood and stone and made idols for themselves, carving them to look like birds and animals and snakes and puny men, and said that these were the great, eternal God, and worshiped them. 24And so God let them go ahead into every sort of sex sin, and do whatever they wanted to; yes, vile and sinful things with each other's bodies.

25Instead of believing what they knew was the truth about God, they deliberately chose to believe lies. So they prayed to the things God made, but wouldn't obey the blessed God who made these things. 26That is why God let go of them and let them do all these evil things, so that even their women turned against God's natural plan for them and indulged in sex sin with each other. 27And the men, instead of having a normal sex relationship with women, burned with lust for each other, men doing shameful things with other men and, as a result, getting paid within their own souls with the wages they so richly deserved.

28So it was that when they gave God up and would not even acknowledge Him, God gave them up to doing everything their evil minds could think of. 29Their lives became full of every kind of wickedness and sin, of greed and hate, envy, murder, fighting, lying, bitterness, and gossip. 30They were backbiters, haters of God, insolent, proud braggarts, always thinking of new ways of sinning and continually disobedient to their parents. 31They tried to misunderstand, broke their promises, and were heartless—without pity.

32They were fully aware of God's death penalty for these crimes, yet they went right ahead and did them anyway, and encouraged others to do them, too.

"Bad Guys" in business suits and loin cloths

What have we here? What a degrading view of humanity. This sounds like a description of the "bad guys," those pagans who have deliberately chosen to push away God's truth.

Well it's true that there is certainly plenty of this kind of thing. This world has its share of atheists and agnostics, and there are just as many pagans wearing business suits as loin cloths. Paul, however, doesn't leave any of these "bad guys" with an excuse. He plainly states that man can know his Creator. Man can see all about him in creation the handiwork of God (v. 20). But instead of acknowledging God, worshiping Him and thanking Him, these pagan reprobates turn from God to themselves. They think up silly ideas of what God is like (v. 23). They turn from the Light and live more and more among the shadows.

11

WE ALL AGREE THAT
THE PAGAN "BAD GUYS"
HAVE PUSHED AWAY
GOD'S TRUTH . . .

And then look at the list of offenses (vs. 24-32): murder, fornication, adultery, homosexuality, greed, hate, envy, lying, etc., etc.

Yes, this is an accurate description. Men have rebelled against God and this is the result. Their selfishness corrupts everything they touch. They see no need to turn to God. What right does God have to their lives? They will do as they please, be their own boss.

And note v. 32. Even though they know of God's death penalty for all these crimes, they go right ahead and do them anyway and even urge others to get in on all the fun. They have drifted so far from God they no longer see or understand the consequences of their actions.

"Well," you may be thinking, "I'm glad that's over. I'm not like that. That kind of people need the gospel, but I fail to see what this has to do with me."

You're not like this? You try to live right? Read on . . .

Romans 2:1-16

¹"Well," you may be saying, "what terrible people you have been talking about!"

But wait a minute!

You are just as bad! When you say they are wicked and should be punished, you are talking about yourself, for you do these very same things. 2And we know that God, in justice, will punish anyone who does such things as these.

3Do you think that God will judge and condemn others for doing them and overlook you when you do them, too? 4Don't you realize how patient He is being with you? Or don't you care? Can't you see that He has been waiting all this time without punishing you to give you time to turn from your sin? His kindness is meant to lead you to repentance. 5But no, you won't listen; and so you are saving up terrible punishment for yourselves because of your stubborn hardness of heart, for there is going to come a day of wrath when God will be the honest Judge of all.

6He will give each one whatever payment he deserves. 7He will give eternal life to those who patiently do the will of God, seeking for glory and honor and for eternal life. 8But He will terribly punish those who fight against the truth of God and walk in evil ways, for God's anger will be poured out upon them.

9There will be sorrow and suffering for Jews and Gentiles alike who keep on sinning. 10But there will be glory and honor and peace from God for all who obey Him, whether they are Jews or Gentiles. 11For God treats everyone the same.

12-15He will punish sin, wherever it is found. He will punish the heathen when they sin, even though they never had God's written laws, for down in their heart they know right from wrong. God's laws are written within them; their own conscience accuses them, or sometimes excuses them. And God will punish the Jews for sinning because they have His written laws but don't obey them. They know what is right but don't

13

do it. After all, salvation is not given to those who know what to do, unless they do it. 16The day will surely come when at God's command Jesus Christ will judge the secret lives of everyone, their inmost thoughts and motives; this is all part of God's great plan which I have already told you about.

We all have some dirty closets

Do you think Paul is fair? How can he say that you do the same things (v. 1) when you try to "live right"?

Though we may see a sin in someone else, we often fail to see the same sin in ourselves. We can point out another's hatred but cannot recognize our own envy. We think someone else has nerve to be bragging all the time, yet fail to detect pride within ourselves.

Therefore Paul now turns his attention to the "good, moral" people who won't listen to God's Word. What does Paul mean? He means that "moral" people keep on thinking of their own goodness and fail to look into their own hearts. He means that they think only of how "nice" they are, and do not consider the Word of God. He means they keep on judging other people, but are blind to their own faults.

Reading between the lines we can imagine Paul thinking about himself as he writes. Before Paul had his life-changing encounter with Christ, he was an "ethical" person who looked down his nose at a bad world. But when he met Christ, Paul began to see himself as he really was on the inside. Then he realized he was no longer blameless.

PAUL SAYS THE
"GOOD, MORAL GUYS"
COMMIT THE SAME SINS
AS THE PAGANS . . .

This can only happen when Christ confronts us. It only happens when we view ourselves in His light. As long as we compare ourselves with others, we think we're pretty good. But when we come into the presence of His perfection, that's a different story.

Our secret lives are laid open before God. And that's rough to take. We wouldn't want other people to know these things about us. We try to appear good before others, to keep up a front. But no matter how well we may think we are fooling them, inside we all have some dirty closets we don't want anybody to discover. In fact, we've locked the doors and thrown away the keys.

God knows all about that. Nothing is hidden from His sight. And therefore these words of judgment and punishment are spoken to convict everyone of his need for Christ. *Everyone* needs the gospel. The pagan "bad guy," the moral "good guy" . . . and yes, Paul even has a few words for the "religious" ones, in fact the most religious ones of all—the Jews. And Paul should know. He was once a "religious Jew" himself, and here is what he says . . .

¹⁷You Jews think all is well between yourselves and God because He gave His laws to you; you brag that you are His special friends. ¹⁸Yes, you know what He wants; you know right from wrong and favor the right because you have been taught His laws from earliest youth. ¹⁹You are so sure of the way to God that you could point it out to a blind man. You think of yourselves as beacon lights, directing men to God. ²⁰You think that you can guide the simple and teach even children the affairs of God, for you really know His laws, which are full of all knowledge and truth.

²¹Yes, you teach others—then why don't you teach yourselves?

You tell others not to steal—do *you* steal?

²²You say it is wrong to commit adultery—Do *you* do it?

You say, "Don't pray to idols," but you rob idol temples, which is just as bad.

²³You are so proud of knowing God's laws, *but you dishonor Him by breaking them.* ²⁴No wonder, as the Scriptures say, the world hates God because of you.

²⁵Being a Jew is worth something if you obey God's laws, but if you don't, then you are no better off than the heathen. ²⁶And if the heathen obey God's laws, won't God give them all the rights and honors He planned to give the Jews? ²⁷In fact, those heathen will be much better off than you Jews who know so much about God and have His promises but don't obey His laws.

²⁸For you are not real Jews just because you were born of Jewish parents or because you have gone through the Jewish initiation ceremony of circumcision. ²⁹No, a real Jew is anyone whose heart is right with God. For God is not looking for those who cut their

bodies in actual body circumcision, but He is looking for those with changed hearts and minds. Whoever has that kind of change in his life will get his praise from God, even if not from you.

The world hates God because of your "religion"

Paul speaks to the Jews of his time. They were religious. They read their Bible regularly. They prayed, fasted, tithed and worshiped God. They were the good, solidly religious people who never questioned their standing with God. It never crossed their minds that they too might be under God's condemnation, but they were.

What had gone wrong? Paul knew. The Jews had grown proud and their pride had led to hypocrisy. They were proud of knowing God's laws, but they dishonored Him by breaking them (v. 23)! Paul even adds this accusation in v. 24: "No wonder, as the Scriptures say, the world hates God because of you!"*

And the same thing happens today. In many churches, religion comes before personal commitment to Christ. Religion can make you proud and self-righteous, but in reality you fail to be kind, honest, humble, loving. Why do so many people stay away from the church? Why do they accuse Christians of hypocrisy? Because they see through the game called "religion," and they call it phony.

Let's be honest about this. It just isn't a case of "sinners who don't want to see the light." True, the

---

*Compare Rom. 2:24 and Isaiah 52:5 in the Authorized Version. Note both verses speak of God's name being blasphemed because of religious hypocrisy.

17

... AND EVEN THE "RELIGIOUS" MAN CAN'T REACH HIGH ENOUGH TO MEET GOD'S STANDARD— A CHANGED MIND AND HEART.

Devil is blinding them, but the religious hypocrisy in the church is hardly helping to make them see.

Paul exposes the failure of "religion" in this passage. He flatly states that no one is free from sin. Even religious people, even the chosen Jews, need a change of mind and heart. That's the only thing that counts.

It's fairly obvious by now that God doesn't grade on any kind of curve. In fact all men fail to get a passing grade. And so Paul sums up God's case against man with this final indictment ...

Romans 3:1-22

¹Then what's the use of being a Jew? Are there any special benefits for them from God? Is there any value in the Jewish circumcision ceremony?
²Yes, being a Jew has many advantages. First of all, God trusted them with His laws (so that they could

18

know and do His will). ³True, some of them were unfaithful, but just because they broke their promises to God, does that mean God will break His promises to those who love Him? ⁴Of course not! Though everyone else in the world is a liar, God is not. Do you remember what the book of Psalms says about this? That God's words will always prove true and right, no matter who questions them.

⁵"But," some say, "our breaking faith with God is good, our sins serve a good purpose, for people will notice how good God is when they see how bad we are. Is it fair, then, for Him to punish us when our sins are helping Him?" (That is the way some people talk.) ⁶God forbid! Then what kind of God would He be, to overlook sin? How could He ever condemn anyone? ⁷For He could not judge and condemn me as a sinner if my dishonesty brought Him glory by pointing up His honesty in contrast to my lies. ⁸If you follow through with that idea you come to this: the worse we are, the better God likes it! But the damnation of those who say such things is just. Yet some claim that this is what I preach!

⁹Well, then, are we Jews *better* than others? No, not at all, for we have already shown that all men alike are sinners, whether Jews or Gentiles.

¹⁰As the Scriptures say, No one is good—no one in all the world.

¹¹No one has ever really known God's way, or even truly wanted to.

¹²Every one has sinned; all are worthless to God. No one anywhere has kept on doing what is right; not one. ¹³Their talk is foul and filthy like the stench from an open grave. Their tongues are loaded with lies. Everything they say has in it the sting and poison of deadly snakes. ¹⁴Their mouths are full of cursing and bitter-

ness. ¹⁵They are quick to kill, hating anyone who disagrees with them. ¹⁶Wherever they go they leave misery and trouble behind them. ¹⁷And they have never known what it is to try to be kind and good. ¹⁸They care nothing about God nor what He thinks of them.

¹⁹So the curse of God lies very heavily upon the Jews, for they are responsible to keep God's laws instead of doing all these evil things; not one of them has any excuse; in fact, all the world stands hushed and guilty before Almighty God.

²⁰So you can see that no one can ever find God's favor by being good enough. For the more we know of God's laws, the clearer it becomes that we don't obey them, for His laws make us see that we are sinners.

²¹⁻²²But now God has shown us a different way to heaven—not by being "good enough" and trying to keep His laws, but by a new way (though not new, really, for the Old Testament told about it long ago). Now God says He will accept us and make us good and bring us to heaven if we trust Jesus Christ to take away our sins. And we all can be saved in this same way, by coming to Christ, no matter who we are or what we have been like.

Nobody bats 1.000

So there you are. This is hardly the way *we* would normally evaluate humanity, but this is *God's* evaluation of us.

Let's sum it all up in baseball language. There are all kinds of ball players in the major leagues. There is the poor player who has a .180 batting average. There is the good player who hits .275. And then there is the batting champ who comes up

NOBODY BATS 1.000

Pagan   Moral   Religious

with an amazing .374. But who bats 1.000? No one —Ruth, DiMaggio, Mays—no one bats 1.000.

God looks at man and sees him stepping up to the plate, grounding out and striking out time and again, even though once in a while he manages to get a double off the boards. Even for the best of us, it's a pretty poor performance. No one bats 1.000.

Therefore the Good News is not only for the "bad guys" who don't measure up. It's for the "good guys" who think they measure up, and for the "religious" who are trying to measure up. How then does this Good News work? What makes the gospel God's power unto salvation?

For further thought

1. Write down your own definition of sin. Do you think some sins are "worse" than others? Why? Does Paul seem to think some sins are worse than others?

2. Do a study of the Biblical definition of sin by summarizing what these verses say about sin: James 4:17; I John 3:4; Gen. 3:6; I Kings 8:46; Prov. 20:9; Isa. 53:6; I John 1:8.

3. Memorize Rom. 1:18. What does "pushing away the truth" have to do with sin?

4. Major Andrian Mikolayev, Russian cosmonaut, was quoted as saying that while he was in orbit, he "didn't see God up there." Astronaut Gordon Cooper, who flew in Faith 7 and later in Gemini 5, says, "I didn't see God either, but I saw many of the wonders he created." Read Rom. 1:18-20. What would you say to the person who says, "There is no God, I can't see Him"?

CHAPTER 3

Are Christians . . .

ON PAROLE or FULLY PARDONED?

Seems like a strange way to put it . . . parole or pardon for the Christian? Well . . . think about it. When a prisoner is pardoned, he is free unconditionally, no strings or red tape attached. But when a man is paroled, there are conditions. He still has to report to his parole officer. He can't go here; he can't go there. He can't do this; he can't do that. Are you getting the point? A lot of Christians live like they are on parole, act like they're on parole, talk like they're on parole. But has *God* put the Christian on parole? That's what matters. Paul's next few lines are some of his most profound, for here in a few bold strokes of the pen is the heart of the Good News . . .

²³Yes, all have sinned; all fall short of God's glorious ideal; ²⁴Yet now God declares that we are good in His eyes if we trust in Jesus Christ, Who freely takes away our sins. ²⁵For God sent Christ Jesus to take the punishment for our sins and end all God's anger against us. He used Christ's blood and our faith to satisfy God's wrath. In this way He was being entirely fair, even though He did not punish those who sinned in olden times. For He was looking forward to the time when Christ would come and take away those sins. ²⁶And now in these days also He can receive sinners in this same way, because Jesus took away their sins. But isn't this unfair for God to let criminals go free, and say that they are good? No, for He does it on the basis of their trust in Jesus Who took away their sins.

²⁷Then what can we boast about doing to earn our salvation?

Nothing at all.

Why?

Because our salvation is not based on our good deeds; it is based on what Christ has done and our faith in Him. ²⁸So it is that we are saved by faith in Christ and not by the good things we do.

²⁹And does God save only the Jews in this way? No, the Gentiles, too, may come to Him in this same manner. ³⁰God treats us all the same; all, whether Jews or Gentiles, are approved if they have faith.

³¹Well then, if we are saved by faith, does this mean that we no longer need obey God's laws? That's what it does NOT mean. In fact, only when we trust Jesus can we truly obey Him.

There is nothing you can do, except . . .

Now you have come to the vital answer Christianity offers to all who have sinned and fallen short. God has provided for our salvation. He came into the world in the person of Jesus Christ and suffered for us on a bloody and terrible cross. God allowed His only Son to take our sin upon Himself so that we could be "justified." Justified?

The key statement in Rom. 3:23-31 is v. 24. You need to go to the Authorized Version to get the full impact. Ken Taylor's beautifully simple *Living Letters* paraphrase doesn't use some key words that are worth a bit of study.

"Being *justified* freely by his *grace* through the *redemption* that is in Christ Jesus . . ." (Rom. 3:24).

To be "justified" before God means that God's justice has been satisfied through the substitutionary death of His Son, Jesus Christ. Christ paid the penalty for our sin, and He also removed the guilt for our sin. This last point—on guilt—is an important fact that many Christians overlook (or never really understand).

For example, you can try to illustrate justification with a traffic ticket. Suppose you have to go to court for speeding. But you do not wind up paying the fine. You learn that it has been paid by someone else—possibly good old dad or rich Uncle Charley. Getting your fine paid by someone else partially explains justification, but God goes one important step further. While the person with a traffic ticket might get his fine paid, it doesn't alter the fact that he is guilty. But when the sinner turns to God through Christ, *his guilt is wiped out along with the penalty!*

In God's eyes, the Christian is completely pardoned for all past sins. God declares "that we are good in His eyes if we trust in Jesus Christ" (v. 24). And not only that, He accepts us, makes us one of the family so to speak—a spiritual son and heir. (See John 1:12, Rom. 8:16.) The Christian can't completely understand it, but he can say: "God looks on me just-as-if-I'd-never-sinned."

How and why can this be? The next key word is the clue. We are justified freely by God's *grace*— His unmerited favor, mercy and love. Again, like justification, you can only try to illustrate grace ...

Grace is like getting two more days to complete an assignment even though you've goofed off for six weeks and missed the deadline.

Grace is like getting a warning from the traffic officer instead of a $50 fine and suspended license.

Grace is getting another chance, even though you haven't earned it or deserved it. (You may not even want it!)

But no earthly analogy really explains God's grace. God's unmerited love and mercy are available to all men, *even those who hate Him*. When a man is truly sorry about his sin, and when he trusts Christ to be his personal Saviour from sin, God freely forgives and accepts him, no matter what he has done. Only God could offer grace like that!

There is one more "rather important" point ...

We are justified freely by God's grace, through the *redemption* that is in Christ Jesus. Redemption involves payment. Redemption means "releasing

GRACE IS LIKE GETTING A WARNING TICKET WHEN YOU DESERVE A SUSPENDED LICENSE.

from bondage by payment of a price." The idea of a ransom is involved.

Do you remember some of the huge ransoms paid to kidnappers? The Lindberghs paid $50,000 in an effort to save their son. The Weyerhausers, timber tycoons in the state of Washington, paid $200,000 for the release of their nine-year-old boy. Frank Sinatra paid $240,000 for the return of Frank, Jr.

But Christ did more than pay a sum of money for our lives. He gave His own life as a ransom to deliver us from the bondage of sin (Mark 10:45).

Man is separated from God—lost. He is a sinner. He is a captive in the hands of the Devil. Jesus came and died to pay the maximum price to buy us back, for we are rightfully His. The price was *His own life*, given on the cross. He purchased us not with silver or gold, but with His own blood. (See Acts 20:28.)

So, what is there left for us to do?

Nothing.

Nothing except to receive God's Good News, believe it, have faith. "Because our salvation is not based on our good deeds; it is based on what Christ has done and our faith in Him" (Rom. 3:27). Faith in Christ changes us and makes us new persons. Faith, as Martin Luther put it, ". . . is a living, daring confidence in God's grace, so sure and certain that a man would stake his life on it a thousand times."

There is no magic in faith. Faith is simply our response to the salvation Christ obtained for us. We now face God unafraid. The penalty and guilt of sin is gone, paid for by God Himself. Religious rites and works do not make us right with God . . . and God doesn't expect them after we come to Christ either. We are *fully pardoned*, even our guilt is gone. We are not "on parole," earning our freedom, continuing to pay the debts for our crimes.

Wait a minute, you say. Does that mean I can live any way I want to and not be concerned about obeying God's laws? As *Living Letters* puts it: "That's what it does NOT mean" (v. 31). Being pardoned by God makes you a new person. You trust Christ for power to live as you should each day. "In fact, only when we trust Jesus can we truly obey Him" (v. 31). You can't trust Christ by "being religious." Trusting and religious self-effort are contradictory terms. To trust Christ is being a Christian *without* being religious.

You see, God has always saved man by faith. Before the law was given through Moses, God called a man named Abraham. He became the father of the Jewish people. God sought out this Abraham, who lived almost 2000 years before Christ, and he responded *by faith* ...

Romans 4:1-25

1-2Abraham was, humanly speaking, the founder of our Jewish nation.

What were his experiences concerning this question of being saved by faith?

Was it because of his good deeds that God accepted him? If so, then he would have something to boast about.

But from God's point of view Abraham had no basis at all for pride. 3For the Scriptures tell us Abraham *believed God,* and that is why God canceled his sins and declared him just and righteous.

4-5But didn't he earn his right to heaven by all the good things he did?

No, for being saved is a gift; if a person could earn it by being good, then it wouldn't be free—but it is! It is *given* to those who do *not* work for it. For God declares sinners to be good in His sight if they have faith in Christ to save them from God's wrath.

6King David spoke of this, describing the happiness of an undeserving sinner who is declared good by God.

⁷"Blessed, and to be envied," he said, "are those whose sins are forgiven and put out of sight.

⁸"Yes, what joy there is for anyone whose sins are no longer counted against him."

⁹Now then, the question: Is this blessing given only to those who have faith in Christ but also keep the Jewish laws, or is the blessing also given to those who do not keep the Jewish rules, but only trust in Christ?

Well, what about Abraham? We say that he received these blessings through his faith.

Was it by faith alone? Or because he also kept the Jewish rules?

¹⁰For the answer to that question, answer this one: *When* did God give this blessing to Abraham? It was *before he became a Jew*—before he went through the Jewish initiation ceremony of circumcision. ¹¹It wasn't until later on, *after* God had promised to bless him *because of his faith,* that he was circumcised. The circumcision ceremony was a sign that Abraham already had faith and that God had already accepted him and declared him just and good in His sight—before the ceremony took place.

So Abraham is an example of those who believe and are saved without obeying Jewish laws.

We see, then, that those who do not keep these rules are justifed by God through faith. ¹²And those who follow these rules and customs and have been circumcised can see that it is not this ceremony that saves them, for Abraham found favor with God by faith alone, before he was circumcised. ¹³So it is clear that God's promise to give the whole earth to Abraham and his descendants was not because Abraham obeyed God's laws but because he trusted God to keep His promise.

¹⁴But if you still claim that God's blessings go to those who are "good enough," then you are saying that

30

God's promises to those who have faith are meaningless, and faith is foolish. 15But the fact of the matter is this: when we try to gain God's blessing and salvation by keeping His laws, we always end up under His anger, for we always fail to keep them. The only way we can keep from breaking laws is not to have any to break!

16So God's blessings are given to us by faith, as a free gift; we are certain to get them whether or not we follow Jewish customs, if we have faith like Abraham's, for Abraham is the father of us all when it comes to these matters of faith. 17That is what the Scriptures mean when they say that God made Abraham the father of many nations. God will accept all people in every nation who trust God as Abraham did. And this promise is from God Himself, Who makes the dead live again and speaks of future events with as much certainty as though they were already past!

18So, when God told Abraham that He would give him a son who would have many children and become a great nation, Abraham believed God even though such a promise just couldn't come to pass! 19And because his faith was strong, he didn't worry about the fact that he was far too old to be a father, at the age of one hundred, and that Sarah his wife, at ninety,* was also much too old to have a baby. 20But Abraham never doubted. He believed God, for his faith and trust were strong, and he praised God for this blessing before it even happened. 21He was completely sure that God was well able to do anything He promised.

22And because of Abraham's faith, God forgave his sins and called him just and good.

23Now this wonderful promise—that he was accepted and approved through his faith—wasn't just for Abraham's benefit. 24It was for us, too, assuring us that

---

*Genesis 17:17

God will accept us in the same way He accepted Abraham—when we believe the promises of God Who brought back Jesus our Lord from the dead.

25He died for our sins and rose again to make us right with God, filling us with God's goodness.

The faith you have is the faith you show

Why does Paul stop to talk about Abraham? He has good reason. He is writing to Jews and Gentiles who have become Christians. He has made the claim (in chapter 3) that faith is central to being justified before God. But what if this faith idea is not in harmony with God's revealed will in the Old Testament? If there is no biblical foundation for the importance of faith, the Jews could claim Paul to be a heretic. If it is possible for others (the Jews) to be justified by works, to be saved by keeping God's law, Christianity is wrong.

Paul doesn't choose Abraham as an example by accident. Abraham was the father of the Jewish nation. (See Gen. 17:1-8.) If Paul can show that Abraham, of all people, was justified by faith (and not by his works), he has made his point: faith is firmly rooted in the Bible, the Old Testament.

And Paul does make his point. Look again at Rom. 4:1-5. Abraham believed God and that is why God cancelled his sins and declared him just and righteous.*

In Romans 4 Paul is saying to read the story of

---

*Read Rom. 4:1-5 and Gen. 15:6 in Authorized Version. Note that Rom. 4:3 is a quote from Gen. 15:6, explaining that Abraham's faith was "counted unto him for righteousness."

Abraham and decide for yourself. Abraham was called by God to leave his home and go to a new land to found the Jewish nation. He *went*. He was told his wife would have a child, even though he and his wife were well past the age for having children. But *he believed*, and Sarah did bear a son.

With Abraham it was all faith. He believed God. He obeyed God. He had faith and he acted on it. He did not simply sit back and do nothing. Faith is response, action. Belief (mental assent) may be for the study, but faith is for the road.

Abraham is a prime example. The faith you have is the faith you show. Faith is not merely head belief. Faith is life lived in a new way—in response to God's revealed will. Faith is practical. Faith is not fantasy. Faith means risk. Abraham went out, not knowing where he was going.

U. S. astronauts, from Glenn and Carpenter on, had a kind of scientific faith. Careful calculations made them believe that things would work out and they blasted off. But Abraham had even greater faith. *He had no way of calculating how things would work out.* He accepted God's Word. He stepped out in trust and obedience. The faith you have is the faith you show. And when you have faith, it does show, as you'll see in the next chapter . . .

For further thought

1. Read Rom. 3:23-26 in different versions and translations. Note that Rom. 3:23, 24 are one thought and should be read together. Compare Rom. 3:24 with

Eph. 1:7; Col. 1:14; Heb. 9:12-15. Write in your own words the importance of the blood of Christ to a Christian's salvation.

2. Memorize Rom. 3:24. Also summarize II Cor. 12:9; Titus 3:5; Phil. 4:19. Write a brief statement of what God's grace means to you.

3. Summarize Gal. 3:24 and Acts 13:39 in your own words. Then write a definition of "justification by faith."

4. Summarize Gal. 3:13; Col. 1:14; Heb. 9:12; I Peter 1:18 in your own words. Then write a definition of "redemption."

CHAPTER 4

Is your faith more than 'fire insurance'?

"Being saved"—justified by faith in Christ—assures us of eternal life. But is that the whole story? A criticism of Christianity is that it just offers "pie in the sky by and by." Christians are accused (and some with good reason) that they get saved in order to take out a "fire insurance policy" against going to hell. But their lives don't show any results. What about this? Does being a Christian provide benefits and results for this life—*right now*?

[1]So, now, since we have been made right in God's sight by faith in His promises, we can have real peace with Him because of what Jesus Christ our Lord has done for us. [2]For because of our faith, He has brought us into this place of highest privilege where we now stand, and we confidently and joyfully look forward to actually becoming all that God has had in mind for us to be.

[3]We can rejoice, too, when we run into problems and trials for we know that they are good for us—they help us learn to be patient. [4]And patience develops strength of character in us and helps us trust God more each time until finally our hope and faith are strong and steady. [5]Then, when that happens, we will be able to hold our heads high no matter what happens and know that all is well, for we will know how dearly God loves us, and we will feel this warm love everywhere within us because God has given us the Holy Spirit to fill our hearts with His love.

[6]When we were utterly helpless with no way of escape, Christ came at just the right time and died for us sinners who had no use for Him.

[7]Even if we were good, we really wouldn't expect anyone to die for us, though of course that might be barely possible. [8]But God showed His great love for us by sending Christ to die for us while we were still sinners.

[9]And since by His blood He did all this for us as sinners, how much more will He do for us now that He has declared us just and good? Now He will save us from all of God's wrath to come. [10]And since, when we were His enemies we were brought back to God by the death of His Son, what blessings He must have for us now that we are His friends, and He is living within

us! 11Now we have the wonderful joy of the Lord in our lives because of what our Lord Jesus Christ has done in dying for our sins and making us His friends.

Real faith brings practical results

What do most people want out of life? Confidence, peace, love, hope, happiness, security, accomplishment. They may express it in different words and ways, but the desires are pretty much the same. In the passage you have just read, Paul claims that the Christian can have all of these things. Being "justified" (made right in God's sight) by faith, gives us real peace with God because of what Jesus Christ our Lord has done for us (v. 1). And, in addition, our faith brings three wonderfully practical results: We have new potential, new power, and a new Friend.

First, the potential. Our faith has brought us into a place of highest privilege and we can confidently look forward to actually becoming all that God has in mind for us to be (v. 2).

"That sounds good," you say, "but how does it work?"

The answer is written all over Romans—have faith, trust God, and obey. God is in charge; let Him do the directing. For example, in order to reach full potential, any great athlete lets his coach direct his training. Bill Glass, great defensive end of the Cleveland Browns and an effective witness for Christ on the football field and off, says that the worst thing that can happen to a player is not to be willing to pay attention to what his coach tells him. "A player," says Glass, "must be able to take coaching and listen to instruction. And when the going gets tough, he must be even more careful about taking the signals of the coach."*

Second, the power. Paul says that Christians can rejoice when problems come because difficulties help them learn to be patient (v. 3). Who wants problems? Nobody, really, but problems come anyway.

Paul, however, sees a problem as something he can use, not something that lays him low. A problem gives you the opportunity to be patient, which develops strength of character. We learn to trust God more and more until our faith is really strong (v. 4).

"All very fine," you may say, "but where is the power? Where do I get all this patience and strength? I have a short fuse and I get discouraged pretty easily at times ... I start out by wanting to trust God. I even pray about it—passing an exam, getting that job, winning that game, making that deadline—but what happens when I don't pass, when I don't make it? What happens when there's just me and the problem?"

For the Christian it is never "just me and the problem." God is there, too. No matter what happens we can know that all is well, that God loves us. Why? Because we can feel his love within us as the Holy Spirit fills our hearts with his love (v. 5).

Here is the first mention of the Holy Spirit in Romans. It won't be the last. The Holy Spirit is the vital key to being a Christian without being reli-

---

*From *Get In the Game* by Bill Glass. Copyright 1966. Word Books.

gious. For the Christian, every trial, every problem can be a useful experience to build his faith, his confidence, his hope, his happiness . . . *if he faces it by relying on the Holy Spirit.*

How does the Christian rely on the Holy Spirit? There are various formulas, but here's one you may not have tried: *Wait. Do nothing.*

"There are times," writes Richard Halverson, "when doing something only compounds the problem, deepens the difficulty, adds to the confusion. Doing nothing is a strategy . . . a conscious, positive, constructive strategy. Leave a glass of muddy water alone—the dirt and debris settles to the bottom. This is a way of purifying water . . . and it's a way of allowing a confused situation to clarify. Waiting brings facts into focus—helps you see them in perspective."*

To wait doesn't mean that you never go into action on a certain problem. But to wait and do nothing in your own strength is a way to rely on the Holy Spirit. Waiting, thinking, praying can give God's love, which is poured into your heart by the Holy Spirit, a chance to calm the troubled waters that are boiling inside. Try it and see how it works.

Third, the Friend. If you wanted to put one thing on the top of the "what I want out of life" heap, it would have to be love. We all want to know that we matter to someone. It can mean the difference between despair and meaningfulness in life.

The Christian knows tha⁺ someone cares. He

---

*From *Perspective*, September 1966, weekly devotional letter by Dr. Richard C. Halverson.

PEACE WITH GOD MEANS POTENTIAL FOR LIFE . . .

FAITH IN CHRIST GIVES POWER TO TAKE IT WHEN THINGS GET TOUGH . . .

I KNOW GOD CARES FOR ME . . .

knows God loves him. God showed his love for us by sending Christ to die for us (v. 8).

The Christian may seem to be alone with his problem, his trials, with his convictions. The Christian may seem small and insignificant, but he has God's Word for it that God cares. As Paul puts it, "Now we have the wonderful joy of the Lord in our lives because of what our Lord Jesus Christ has done in dying for our sins and making us His friends" (v. 11).

Is your faith more than fire insurance? It should be. It better be. If it isn't, perhaps you are only going through the motions ... perhaps you are trying to be a Christian by being ... "religious."

Paul seems to digress a bit in the rest of chapter 5, or is he just expanding the incredible concept of how "while we were yet sinners Christ died for us"? Here is profound thinking on man's sin and God's mercy ...

Romans 5:12-21

12When Adam sinned, the entire human race was declared guilty. His sin brought death into the world, and so everything began to grow old and die. 13We know that it was Adam's sin that caused this— and not each person dying because of his own sins— because although of course people were sinning from the time of Adam until Moses, God did not in those days judge them guilty of death for breaking His laws —because He had not yet given His laws to them, nor told them what He wanted them to do. 14So when they died it was not for these sins of their own; and since they themselves had never disobeyed God's special law against eating the forbidden fruit, as Adam had, their dying was not because of that. It was because, when Adam sinned, all of us were declared guilty with him and began to die because of his sin.

What a contrast between Adam and Christ Who was yet to come. 15And what a difference between man's sin and God's forgiveness. For this one man, Adam, brought death to many through his *sin*. But this one man, Jesus Christ, brought forgiveness to many through God's *mercy*. 16Adam's *one* sin brought the penalty of death to many, while Christ freely takes away *many* sins and gives glorious life instead. 17The sin of this one man, Adam, caused *death to be king over all*, but all who will take God's gift of forgiveness and approval are *kings of life* because of this one man, Jesus Christ. 18Yes, Adam's *sin* brought *punishment* to all, but Christ's act of *goodness* makes men *right with God*, so that they can live. 19Adam caused many to be sinners because he *disobeyed* God, and Christ caused many to be made acceptable to God because He *obeyed*.

20The Ten Commandments were given so that all could see the extent of their failure to obey God's laws. But the more we see our sinfulness, the more we see God's abounding grace forgiving us.

21And so sin ruled over all men and brought them to death, but now God's kindness rules instead, giving us right standing with God and resulting in eternal life through Jesus Christ our Lord.

Adam and Christ: a world of difference

"How can Jesus save us all?" you may ask. "How can one die for so many?"

Look at it this way:

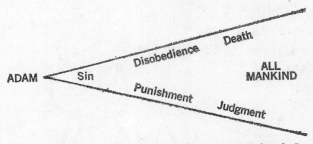

One man, Adam, brought all this on mankind. So also this One, who is the eternal Son of God, has power to bring life to all who believe:

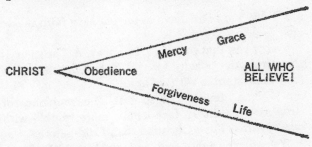

For further thought

1. Compare Rom. 5:2 (*Living Letters*) with Eph. 3:16-21. How can you become the person God has in mind for you to be? List some specific steps.

2. Review the cartoons on p. 40, which illustrate how faith in Christ offers the Christian potential, power, and the assurance that he is not alone, that he has a Friend who loves him. Pick the cartoon that says the most to you and explain why.

3. Memorize Rom. 5:2 in the *Living Letters* paraphrase and then write a brief paper on "My faith is more than fire insurance because":

CHAPTER 5

Whose slave are you?

"Why, I'm not a slave to anyone. My faith makes me free!"

Why, yes, that's right ... in a way. A Christian is free from the penalty for sin. In fact, he never has any more trouble with sin at all ...

"Wait a minute; not so fast. I have plenty of trouble with sin. In fact I have more trouble with sin now that I'm a Christian than I did before."

Yes, that's right, too, and Paul had the same experience. So it is *sin in the Christian's daily life* that Paul writes about as he starts Romans 6. He has already explained "justification by faith." Now he's going on to the subject that separates the religious striver from the trusting believer ... sanctification. People shy away from a word like "sanctification." It sounds so formidable, so pious. What does it mean? Paul knew ... and in these next pages of his letter he wrestles with the fact that a person *can't* be a Christian by being religious. Mere religion, you see, is not enough ...

1Well then, shall we keep on sinning so that God can keep on showing us more and more kindness and forgiveness?

2-3Of course not!

Should we keep on sinning when we don't have to? For sin's power over us was broken when we became Christians and were baptized to become a part of Jesus Christ: through His death the power of your sinful nature was shattered. 4Your old sin-loving nature was buried with Him by baptism when He died, and when God the Father, with glorious power, brought Him back to life again, you were given His wonderful new life to enjoy.

5For you have become a part of Him, and so you died with Him, so to speak, when He died; and now you share His new life, for you have risen with Him when He rose. 6Your old evil desires were nailed to the cross with Him; that part of you that loves to sin was crushed and fatally wounded, so that your sin-loving body is no longer under sin's control, no longer needs to be a slave to sin; 7for when you are deadened to sin you are freed from all its allure and its power over you. 8And since your old sin-loving nature "died" with Christ, we believe that you are now sharing His new life.

9Christ rose from the dead and will never die again. Death no longer has any power over Him.

10He died once for all to end sin's power, but now He lives forever in unbroken fellowship with God. 11So look upon your old sin nature as dead and unresponsive to sin and be alive instead to God, alert to Him, through Jesus Christ our Lord. 12Do not let sin control you any longer; do not obey it; do not submit to it by giving in to its desires. 13Do not let any part of your bodies become tools of wickedness, to be used for sinning; but give yourselves completely to God—every part of you—for you are back from death and you want to be tools in the hands of God, to be used for His good purposes.

¹⁴Sin need never again be your master, for now you are no longer tied to the law where sin enslaves you, but you are free under God's favor and mercy.

¹⁵So now shall we sin and not worry about it? (For our salvation does not depend on keeping the law, but on receiving God's grace!)

Of course not!

¹⁶Don't you realize that you can choose your own master? You can choose sin (with death) or else obedience (with goodness). The one to whom you offer yourself, he will take you and be your master and you will be his slave. ¹⁷Thank God that though you once chose to be slaves of sin, now you are obeying with all your heart the teaching to which God has committed you. ¹⁸And now you are free from your old master, sin; and you have become slaves to your new master, goodness and righteousness.

¹⁹I speak this way, using the illustration about slaves, because it makes it easy to understand: just as you used to be slaves to all kinds of sin, so now you must let yourselves be slaves to all that is right and holy. ²⁰In those days when you were slaves of sin you didn't bother much with goodness.

²¹And what was the result?

Evidently not good, since you are ashamed now even to think about those things you used to do, for they ruined you.

²²But now you are free from the power of sin and are slaves of God, and His benefits to you include holiness and everlasting life.

²³For the wages of sin is death, but the free gift of God is eternal life through Jesus Christ our Lord.

You belong to your choice

"Well, I can't be perfect anyway. So what if I sin a little? God will forgive me."

Ever get an idea like that? It's a typical trap for any Christian, for as any Christian knows, "getting saved" doesn't solve all your problems with sin. You are saved from the *penalty* and *guilt* of sin—"justified by faith" as Paul explained it in Romans 3 and 4. But the *power* of sin is still there, working on you, tempting you. The natural conclusion, then, is to let the "slips befall you where they may." There is always I John 1:9. Confess. God is faithful. He forgives and cleanses. And soon it becomes a kind of game, but you never win, and you don't feel right about it.

Paul deals briefly with this idea of "let's sin all the more, so God can show all the more grace and mercy." He says, "God forbid!" And then he comes up with more good news about the Good News. We don't have to keep on sinning, because sin's power over us was broken when we became Christians.

Sin's power broken? It doesn't seem that way. Why do Christians still have so many temptations? And why do they still sin?

Paul sails into some deep water in Romans 6. He is drawing pictures with words, symbolizing what happens when a person becomes a Christian. The Christian becomes a part of Christ, and so the Christian figuratively "dies" with Christ as He died on the cross. And, the Christian also rises with Christ, as He rose from the grave.

Hard to understand? Yes, but this is another vital key to the difference between "religion" and Christianity. A Christian is not someone who simply follows Christ's great teachings. A Christian is one who is *one with Christ* in a *personal* relationship. That is why Paul says in v. 6: "Your old evil desires were nailed to the cross with Him; that part of you that loves to sin was crushed and fatally wounded, so that your sin-loving body is no longer under sin's control, no longer needs to be a slave to sin."

My evil desires nailed to the cross? That part of me that loves to sin fatally wounded? It doesn't seem that way to me . . .

Perhaps it doesn't. But the key to this passage is to remember that Paul is painting a picture, and *it's the way you want to look at that picture that makes the difference.*

So, look at it this way. Paul is saying that becoming a Christian means that you not only start to follow Christ, but *you also identify with Him, you become part of Him.* And just as Christ conquered the power of sin with His death and resurrection, Christ also struck a telling blow against the old, sinful nature that is part of every one of us.

The question is, do you want to let that telling blow work in your favor or do you want to still fight your own battles? This is the paradox. Christ doesn't force His way into your life. He doesn't walk in and say, "I'm taking over. From now on you do things my way, or else." He gives you a choice. You are no longer under sin's complete

**IF A CHRISTIAN COULDN'T BE TEMPTED,
HE WOULD BE A ROBOT . . .**

domination, but neither are you a robot. (Robots don't get tempted, but they don't experience love, joy, peace and satisfaction either.)

So Paul says that we should "reckon" (look upon) our old sinful nature as dead. In other words, we *really believe* that "sin's fangs have been pulled" and that we are alive to God, alert to Him through Jesus Christ our Lord.

Paul never claims that the Christian is free from temptation, impervious to sin, sealed in a plastic coating called "salvation." Temptations to sin still come, but what Paul is driving at is that *now you don't have sin as your only alternative.* Another route is open—obedience to Christ. The choice is yours.

Choice is always a part of life. And with every choice you make you are actually turning toward sin or Christ. There is no middle, "neutral" ground.

You do not remain the same. You are always changing.

And you become like the one you obey. If you serve sin, it means frustration, disillusionment, a kind of cynical hardening toward the gospel. But if you serve Christ, He molds your life. The one to whom you offer yourself will take you and be your master and you will be his slave. *And you become like the one to whom you belong!*

And so we choose one of two masters. We serve God or sin. Some think that while they may "sin a little," they are still master of a particular habit or practice. It doesn't work out that way. You don't master a sin; it masters you. *You belong to the power you choose to obey.* You accept Christ by faith, but unless your faith in Him is constant and real, sin will still rule your life.

You see, there are three aspects to sanctification: positional, experiential and ultimate.

Positional sanctification means every believer is "sanctified" in the sense that he is in the position of being one with Christ. Paul even said that those who were living in carnal sin in the church at Corinth were "sanctified saints" (I Cor. 6:11).

Ultimate sanctification refers to heaven, eternal life. It is another term for glorification, that is, being like Christ at His coming (I John 3:1-3).

But what Paul is directly concerned with in Romans 6 is experiential sanctification, actually experiencing triumph over sin in your daily life.

We can define sanctification in neat theological terms: "a setting apart for use by God through holy living in accordance with God's will." But perhaps

50

this ponderous word has more meaning when seen simply as "letting Christ make a real difference in your life." The only way there can be a "real difference" is that we be able to freely choose our own master. Without the element of choice, our sanctification would be a sterile mechanical thing. We would be "justified computers." But God doesn't want computers. He wants Christians who see themselves as dead to sin and alive to Him, through Jesus Christ.

Whose slave are you? Go back to Rom. 6:11. *It all depends on how you choose to look at living the Christian life.* "Being religious" doesn't help here. You are a part of Christ, but you have a choice: sin or obedience to Him. *You belong to your choice.*

Paul isn't through with showing that the Christian life is a personal relationship to Christ. In Rom. 7:1-14 he uses marriage to illustrate the bond between the Christian and his Lord. The Christian is no longer married to the law because he has died to sin and dissolved that contract. The Christian is now married, so to speak, to Christ . . .

Romans 7:1-14

¹Don't you understand yet, dear Jewish brothers in Christ, that when a person dies the law no longer holds him in its power?

²Let me illustrate: when a woman marries, the law binds her to her husband as long as he is alive. But if he dies, she is no longer bound to him. The laws of marriage no longer apply to her. ³Then she can marry someone else if she wants to. That would be wrong

while he was alive, but it is perfectly all right after he dies.

⁴Your "husband," your master, used to be the Jewish law; but you "died," as it were, with Christ on the cross; and since you are "dead," you are no longer "married to the law," and it has no more power over you. Then you came back to life again when Christ did, and are a new person. And now you are "married," so to speak, to the One who rose from the dead, so that you can produce good fruit, that is, good deeds for God.

⁵When your old nature was still active, sinful desires were at work within you, making you want to do whatever God said not to, and producing sinful deeds, the rotting fruit that comes with death. ⁶But now you need no longer worry about the Jewish laws and customs because you "died" while in their captivity, and now you can really serve God; not in the old way, mechanically obeying a set of rules, but in the new way, with all of your hearts and minds.

⁷Well then, am I suggesting that these laws of God are evil?

Of course not!

No, the law is not sinful but it was the law that showed me my sin. I would never have known the sin in my heart—the evil desires that are hidden there—except the law said, "You must not have evil desires in your heart." ⁸But sin used this law against evil desires by reminding me that such desires are wrong and arousing all kinds of forbidden desires within me! Only if there were no laws to break would there be no sinning.

⁹That is why I felt fine so long as I did not understand what the law really demanded. But when I found out then I realized that I had broken the law and was a sinner, doomed to die. ¹⁰So, as far as I was

concerned, the good law which was supposed to show me the way of life resulted instead in my being given the death penalty. [11]Sin fooled me by taking the good laws of God and using them to make me guilty of death. [12]So you see the law itself is wholly right and good.

[13]But didn't the law cause my doom? How then can it be good?

No, it was sin, devilish stuff that it is, that used what was good to bring about my condemnation. So you can see from the way sin uses God's good laws for its own evil purposes, how cunning and deadly and damnable it is. [14]The law is good. The trouble is not there, but with *me*, because I am too sinful to obey it.

The problem is not with the law

Paul wants to clarify an important point right here. He opens up by saying that the Christian is no longer married to the law. He has "died" as far as the law is concerned and is now one with Christ. But Paul doesn't want you to get the idea that the law is something evil. The real enemy is sin— damnable stuff that uses God's good laws for its own evil purposes.

Paul knows that the trouble is not in the law; the trouble is in him ... as he will show in the next part of his letter ...

For further thought

1. Compare Rom. 6:1-11 with Eph. 4:20-32 and Col. 4:1-17. Then write your own concept of what it means to be "dead to sin and alive to God."

2. Review Rom. 6:19-23. How do you feel about

being a slave to God? How do you reconcile this idea with John 8:32?

3. Why does Christ leave the Christian with a choice between sin and following Him? Why doesn't God control the Christian so completely that he could never sin?

4. Memorize Rom. 6:16. Do you agree with the statement in this chapter that if you "play around with sin" you don't master it; it masters you? Can you think of any personal experiences that bear this out?

CHAPTER 6

How do I win the war within?

The Spirit vs. Self...

Romans 6 was "good for openers" on this problem of sin in a Christian's life, but you probably want to know a lot more. What's your problem? Temper? Impatience? Self-control? Sex? Being honest? Your thought life? Pride? Laziness? Self-centeredness? Everyone has his skeletons, and they don't always stay in the closet. You want to do right but you do wrong. You want to choose obedience but you choose sin. Sometimes you'd almost swear you were a split personality, a regular "walking civil war." Read on. Paul admits that he fights that war, too . . .

¹⁵I don't understand myself at all, for I really want to do what is right, but I can't. I do what I don't want to—what I hate. ¹⁶I know perfectly well that what I am doing is wrong and that the laws I am breaking are good ones. ¹⁷But I can't help myself because I'm not doing it. It is sin inside me that is stronger than I am that makes me do these evil things. ¹⁸I know I am rotten through and through so far as my old sinful nature is concerned. No matter which way I turn I can't make myself do right. I want to but I can't. ¹⁹When I want to do good, I don't; and when I try not to do wrong, I do it anyway. ²⁰Now if I am doing what I don't want to, it is plain where the trouble is: sin still has me in its evil grasp. ²¹It seems to be a fact of life that when I want to do what is right, I inevitably do what is wrong. ²²I love to do God's will so far as my new nature is concerned; ²³but there is something else deep within me, in my lower nature, that is at war with my mind and wins the fight and makes me a slave to the sin and death that are still within me. In my mind I want to be God's willing servant but instead I find myself still enslaved to sin. ²⁴⁻²⁵So you see how it is: my new life tells me to do right, but the old nature that is still inside me loves to sin.

Oh, what a terrible thing this is!

Who will free me from my slavery to this deadly lower nature? Thank God! It has been done through Jesus Christ our Lord.

He has set me free.

How do I get out of this mess

Does Paul's struggle sound familiar? We all experience the frustration of knowing what is right and failing to do it. This isn't supposed to be the Christian's experience, but Rom. 7:15-24 draws an accurate picture of the vicious circle we all get into.

I start the day with devotions and feel pretty good . . .

But in no time at all I hit a snag. I run smack into trouble . . . somebody I don't like, a situation I can't handle, a nice juicy temptation . . .

I know I shouldn't let this thing get to me this way. After all, it's not a good testimony . . .

But no matter which way I turn, or how hard I try ...

I flub it, wind up defeated, tied in knots, a slave to sin ...

And my question is ... how do I get out of this mess? If I'm a Christian, why can't I lick this thing???

So we may as well be honest. This "new life in Christ" is no snap. We come to Christ as sinners. We are saved by God's amazing grace. We are forgiven and justified before God. *But we are still sinners after we believe.* Paul found this out. He

58

admitted that he was "rotten through and through" (v. 18).

The inescapable fact is that by ourselves we can't do the right thing. We just don't make it. Knowing the rules, golden or otherwise, doesn't make us able to obey. We keep on falling into the trap called sin, *because we choose to.* The old nature is still in every Christian, trying to keep the new nature from taking over. And there is no "peaceful co-existence." The Christian is a "walking civil war."

Paul has the answer to winning this war. First you have to be sure you understand who is fighting it, and then you need good military strategy. Here is his battle plan . . .

Romans 8:1-17

1So there is no condemnation awaiting those who belong to Christ Jesus.

2For the power of the life-giving Spirit—and this power is mine through Christ Jesus—has freed me from the vicious circle of sin and death.

3We aren't saved from sin's grasp by knowing the commandments of God, because we can't and don't keep them, but God put into effect a different plan to save us. He sent His own Son, in a human body like ours—except that ours are sinful—and destroyed sin's control over us by giving Himself as a sacrifice for our sins.

4So now we can obey God's laws if we follow after the Holy Spirit and no longer obey the old evil nature within us.

5Those who let themselves be controlled by their lower natures live only to please themselves; but those who follow after the Holy Spirit find themselves doing those things that please God.

⁶Following after the Holy Spirit leads to life and peace, but following after the old nature leads to death, ⁷because the old sinful nature within us is against God. It never did obey God's laws and it never will.

⁸That's why those who are still under the control of their old sinful selves, bent on following their old evil desires, can never please God.

⁹But you are not like that.

You are controlled by your new nature if you have the Spirit of God living in you. (And remember that if anyone doesn't have the Spirit of Christ living in him, he is not a Christian at all.) ¹⁰Yet, even though Christ lives within you, your body will die because of sin; but your spirit will live, for Christ has made it just and good. ¹¹And if the Spirit of God, Who raised up Jesus from the dead, lives in you, He will make your dying bodies live again after you die, by means of this same Holy Spirit living within you.

¹²So, dear brothers, you have no obligations whatever to your old sinful nature to do what it begs you to do. ¹³For if you keep on following it you are lost and will perish, but if through the power of the Holy Spirit you crush it and its evil deeds, you will live. ¹⁴For all who are led by the Spirit of God are sons of God.

¹⁵And so we should not be like cringing, fearful slaves, but we should behave like God's very own children, adopted into the bosom of His family, and calling to Him, "Father, Father." ¹⁶For His Holy Spirit speaks to us deep in our hearts, and tells us that we really are God's children.

¹⁷And since we are His children, then we will share His treasures—for all God gives His Son Jesus is ours now too. But we must also share His suffering if we are to share His glory.

So we "have the Holy Spirit." You've probably heard that before. It's a nice, comfortable, "spiritual" thought.

But what does it mean? Paul says: ". . . the power of the life-giving Spirit . . . has freed me from the vicious circle of sin and death."

What is Paul saying? Didn't he just get through admitting that he couldn't make the grade, that he couldn't obey the law, good as the law might be? Yes, that's the point. When we try to obey the law, we are trying to do something for God. But when we follow after the Holy Spirit (vs. 4,5), *we let God do something for us.*

Some Christians fail because they don't even know they have the Holy Spirit within them. But perhaps a lot more Christians fail because the concept of the Holy Spirit within is only that—a nice idea, a pat theological cliche that doesn't have a thing to do with their real lives.

But the Holy Spirit is not just a "concept." He is a Person. He is the Spirit of Christ and He does have something to do with your life, especially if you're interested in living a Christian life, not just being "religious."

Look at it this way. If you are a Christian, you have a battle on your hands. You are constantly facing a choice between sin and obedience. The fact that you are aware of the choice, that you are concerned, shows that you want to win this war within. But how badly do you want to win it? In the 1950's and '60's the United States fought "small

61

wars" that it didn't really try to win. Containment was more of a goal than all out victory. A "peaceful settlement" was preferable to unconditional surrender.

You can't fight that kind of war with sin. It will whip you every time. You have to decide which way you really want to go . . .

You say you want to live for Christ, do the right thing . . .

But, there's one big problem, isn't there? You are fighting this war with a reservation. You don't really want to win it, because that would mean you couldn't be in charge. But in this war, no Christian is a general. All of us are non-coms, and our orders are to . . . follow after the Holy Spirit.

Paul puts the choice to you quite clearly in Rom. 8:5: "Those who let themselves be controlled by their lower natures live only to please themselves; but

ALL RIGHT, LORD, I'LL TAKE YOUR ROUTE.

those who follow after the Holy Spirit find themselves doing those things that please God." And you know, it's a funny thing . . . when you wind up pleasing God, you please yourself, too. Christ conquers sin and you win that war within.

"All very true," you say. "Sounds good, but can I have a few practical instructions? Any examples you can give me of how to do this?"

First, get a good picture of the kind of war you're fighting. You are the battleground. The opposing forces are the Spirit and the self (human nature, ego). "These two forces within us are constantly fighting each other to win control over us and our wishes are never free from their pressures" (Gal. 5:17, *Living Letters*).

Next, realize you don't fight this war by dashing around saying, "I'm gonna be good, I'm gonna be good . . . I'll think good thoughts, etc." This is a foot soldier war. You fight it by *walking*. And there are only two ways to walk: in the Spirit, or in the flesh (going your own merry way). When Paul talks about walking and following after the Spirit, he suggests continuous action and motion. The Christian life is not simply a Sunday stroll with Jesus. It's a daily choice, a daily commitment to follow the

**SELF VS. SPIRIT
FACT OF THE CHRISTIAN LIFE**

Spirit, or a daily surrender to pleasing the old me, the sinful self.

For an example of walking in the Spirit, try Vonda Kay Van Dyke, Miss America of 1965. Moments before stepping on stage for the final judging, she prayed that she might perform to the best of her ability and, if possible, witness for Christ.

She got her chance. Emcee Bert Parks queried, "I understand you always carry a Bible with you as a good-luck charm. Tell us about your religion."

"I don't consider my Bible a good-luck charm," replied Vonda Kay. "It is the most important book I own. I would not describe my companionship with God as a religion, but as a faith. I believe in Him, trust in Him, and pray that ... His will may be done."*

Exactly how was this an example of "walking in the Spirit"? Examine the situation again. Vonda Kay prayed. (You can't walk with the Spirit and not be on speaking terms.) She asked for opportunity to show her loyalty to Christ. (You don't walk with

*From *That Girl in Your Mirror* by Vonda Kay Van Dyke. Copyright 1966. Fleming H. Revell Company. Used by permission.

the Spirit and deny His cause.) When the test came, she had power to meet it. (The Scriptures say that the Spirit will teach us what to say and bring it to mind when it's needed. See John 14:26.)

Vonda Kay Van Dyke's success sounds fine, but you may be wondering what to do if things don't work out quite so nicely for you.

It seems more your luck to have someone say, "I understand you read the Bible and other fairy tales."

To which you brilliantly reply: "Daaaa, Oh, why don't you drop dead?"

Half an hour later, of course, you have worked out a precise statement that is a combination of clever wit and wholesome witness, but by then your friend (and the opportunity) is long gone. Does your attack of "slow witness" and quick temper mean that you can never hope to walk in the Spirit?

Hardly. The realistic Christian is ready for momentary defeats, *but he never goes into permanent retreat.* It would take a perfect person to continually walk in the Spirit without one misstep. Perfect people are in short supply this side of eternity.

The thing to do is to start each day with a definite decision that, *by faith,* you will walk in the Spirit and not live only to please yourself. When you sin, confess it on the spot if you can remember to do so. *And keep going.* Many a Christian's walk in the Spirit becomes a self-centered sojourn because he doesn't have the backbone to admit to God (and others) that he's wrong, pick things up and go on from there. If you really want to walk in the Spirit, no one is standing in your way but yourself. Go ahead and take the first step . . .

The Holy Spirit does still more for the Christian. Through the Spirit the Christian has hope. Life is not a dead-end street. The Christian looks forward to the day when even his body will no longer be victim to decay, death. He will have a new body, a body that will never die . . .

Romans 8:18-27

[18]Yet what we suffer now is nothing compared to the glory He will give us later. [19]For all creation is waiting patiently and hopefully for that future day when God will glorify His children.* [20-21]For on that day thorns and thistles, sin, death, and decay that overcame the world against its will at God's command will all disappear, and the world around us will share in the glorious freedom from sin which God's children enjoy. [22]For we know that even the things of nature, like animals and plants, groan in sickness and death as they await this great event. [23]And even we Christians, although we have the witness of the Holy Spirit within us, aren't free from trouble; we too wait anxiously for that day when God will give us our full rights as His children, including the new bodies He has promised us —bodies that will not be sick again and that will never die.

[24]We are saved by trusting. And trusting means looking forward to getting something we don't have now; (for a man who already has something doesn't

*literally: "waiting for the revelation of the Sons of God".

need to hope and trust that he will get it).

25But if we must keep trusting God for something that hasn't happened yet, it teaches us to wait patiently and confidently.

26And in the same way—by faith—the Holy Spirit helps us with our daily problems and in our praying. For we don't even know what we should pray for, nor how to pray as we should; but the Holy Spirit prays for us with such feeling that it cannot be expressed in words. 27And the Father Who knows all hearts knows of course what the Spirit is saying as He pleads for us in harmony with God's own will.

Your problems and His problems

The Christian can face the future unafraid. He has more than a set of religious precepts. He is related to the living God.

God's Holy Spirit is already at work within you. He even prays for you. Your daily problems are no longer yours alone. He is there with you all the time—if you will only give Him complete control . . .

For further thought

1. Does the dilemma that Paul describes in Rom. 7:15-21 ring true in your own experience? (Also see cartoons, pp. 57, 58.) Can you see a particular area of your life where you have a particularly difficult time in doing what you want to do or in not doing what you don't want to do?

2. Memorize Rom. 8:5 in *Living Letters* paraphrase. Compare Rom. 8:1-11 with Gal. 5:16-25. Then write a brief statement of the difference between being a Christian (walking in the Spirit) and being religious (being controlled by your ego, in actually living to

please yourself). Note especially Gal. 5:16-18 in *Living Letters*. Should the Christian have to force himself to obey God's Laws? Why?

3. Try experimenting with Gal. 5:16-25. Note the impure results of living only for yourself in vs. 19-21: "But when you follow your own wrong inclinations your lives will produce these evil results: impure thoughts; eagerness for lustful pleasure; idolatry; spiritism (that is, encouraging the activity of demons); hatred and fighting; jealousy and anger; constant effort to get the best for yourself; complaints and criticisms; the feeling that everyone else is wrong except those in your own little group; and there will be wrong doctrine, envy, murder, drunkenness, wild parties and all that sort of thing" (*Living Letters*).

Do any of these areas pertain to you and the way you live? Be honest and specific about yourself, not fuzzy and pseudo spiritual. Make a daily commitment to walk in the Spirit *by faith*, not sight (or your own savoir faire). See how many of these impure results of selfish living are turned into the positive fruit mentioned in vs. 22,23: "But when the Holy Spirit controls our lives He will produce this kind of fruit in us: love, joy, peace, patience, kindness, goodness, faithfulness, gentleness and self-control . . ." (*Living Letters*).

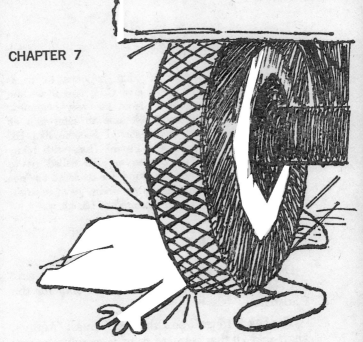

CHAPTER 7

How can ALL things work together for good?

Yes, how can they? Christians love to quote this verse—to *other* people who have troubles. But how many of us really believe it? How many have put Rom. 8:28 to a test, or (more correctly) have been tested by it? How can death, accidents, personal failures and predicaments "work for your good"? Is this just Christian "sour grapes" or "sweet lemon" rationalizing? Before deciding, look more closely at what Paul actually says ...

[28]And we know that all that happens to us is working for our good if we love God, and if we are fitting into His plans. [29]For from the very beginning God decided that those who came to Him—and all along He knew who would—should become like His Son, so that His Son would be the first, with many brothers. [30]And having chosen us, He called us to come to Him; and when we came, He declared us "not guilty," filled us with Christ's goodness, gave us right standing with Himself, and promised us His glory.

Not "Why" but "To What End"?

Does Rom. 8:28 make sense for the Christian? Perfect sense. In fact, it makes sense *only* for the Christian.

The key is to read past the first phrase: "And we know that all that happens to us is working for our good *if we love God* ..." There is the first condition. Loving God is something a Christian certainly wants to do. "We love him, because he first loved us" (I John 4:19). Problem is, it's easier to love God when things are going well than when things are going wrong. In fact, perhaps that is a good test ... just how much do I love God when the going gets rough? Do I let circumstances get the best of me?

Instead of loving God and trusting Him when things go wrong, I can always resort to self-pity. There is nobody I would rather feel sorry for than myself. But feeling sorry for myself doesn't get me anywhere.

HOW TO LET LIFE GET YOU DOWN

"Poor me. How could this happen to such a nice guy?"

FEEL SORRY FOR YOURSELF . . .

"Nobody cares. Nobody understands. Into every life a little rain must fall, but this is too much."

GET DISCOURAGED . . .

"I never get the breaks. Life is a joke and I'm the punch line."

BE BITTER . . .

Is Rom. 8:28 trying to tell me that God is *in my circumstances*? He has allowed this thing to happen, this disappointment, this frustration, perhaps even a tragedy. But if I know that God loves me and I love Him, then my question is not "why," but "to what end?"

But perhaps I decide not to feel mere self-pity over circumstances. I can always give way to discouragement. Everything is going against me. The ball just isn't bouncing my way. Nobody understands. Nobody cares about what I am trying to do. Nobody wants to help.

Nobody? Rom. 8:28 says, ". . . if we love God." I John 4:19 says that we love God because He first loved us. And so here I am — my circumstances, myself and God. Here is where "religion" is not enough. I need a Person, Someone who understands, who cares, who

71

will help me up off the floor to try again. Christ is ready to do this . . . if I am willing to respond to His love with love and trust of my own.

But of course if I really want to go "down the tube" of circumstances, I can become bitter. You've met people who are bitter. Life has played a dirty trick on them. They just didn't get the breaks. When a Christian becomes bitter against life, against the church, even against God, he cuts himself off from the resource he needs most: knowing that God loves him and will help him.

There is more to Rom. 8:28. All things work for our good ". . . if we are fitting into His plans."

And just what are His plans? Go on to v. 29: God's purpose is that we ". . . become like His Son." This doesn't mean you are to become some kind of celestial carbon copy. God always gives freedom to choose, to be an individual, a person. But God also knows our weaknesses, our problems —our sins. He sends circumstances into our lives, circumstances that work much as a sculptor works on stone—chipping away that temper, trimming away the pride, the deceit, the jealousy. Each Christian is a different creation, but God works on us all, *for our good*, with His Son as the model.

When you read Rom. 8:28 in context, you begin to see how all things *do* work together for good. No matter what happens, we know that behind it is God's plan, purpose, and above all His love. Paul goes on to talk about that love as he brings Romans 8 to a climax. He has left the Death Valley of Romans 7 far behind. He's about to finish scaling a spiritual peak that towers higher than Mt. Everest.

Through Christ, Paul knows that he is more than a conqueror ...

Romans 8:31-39

31What can we ever say to such wonderful things as these? If God is on our side, who can ever be against us? 32Since He did not even spare His own Son for us but gave Him up for us all, won't He also surely give us everything else?

33Who dares accuse us whom God has chosen for His own?

Will God?

No! He is the One Who has forgiven us and given us right standing with Himself. 34Who then will condemn us?

Will Christ?

NO! For He is the One Who died for us and came back to life again for us and is sitting at the place of highest honor next to God, pleading for us there in heaven. 35Who then can ever keep away Christ's love from us? When we have trouble or calamity, when we are hunted down or destroyed, is it because He doesn't love us anymore? And if we are hungry, or penniless, or in danger, or threatened with death, has God deserted us? 36No, for the Scriptures tell us that for His sake we must be ready to face death at every moment of the day—we are like sheep awaiting slaughter; 37but despite all this, overwhelming victory is ours through Christ Who loves us.

38For I am convinced that nothing can ever separate us from His love. Death can't, and life can't. The angels won't, and all the powers of hell itself cannot keep God's love away. Our fears for today, our worries about tomorrow. 39Or where we are—high above the sky, or in the deepest ocean—nothing will ever be able to separate us from the love of God that is in Christ Jesus, our Lord.

The Greatest Power We Know!

Can you believe this? Will you believe this? If you will, God can change your life. You will be able to live confidently no matter what tests may come your way. No matter what happens, nothing can change God's love for you. That's worth thinking about when danger, trouble, accident, or death strike. Sometimes Christians feel that they should be delivered from accidents, sickness and death. And when troubles come, they ask: "Why did God let this happen to me?"

The Bible does not promise escape from suffering. If it did, then everybody would become a Christian—just to avoid accidents, troubles, heart attacks, cancer. That might be a good motive for being religious, but it's a poor motive for being a Christian.

Instead God offers us His presence in all of life's troubles. He tells us that nothing can ever shake His love for us. For the Christian, every cloud doesn't have a silver lining, *but behind the clouds the sun is always shining.*

Prose really can't do these last lines of Romans 8 justice, but perhaps the following poetry* by Ralph Carmichael begins to catch the substance of Paul's thought ...

We Are More Than Conquerors

We are more than conquerors through
Him that loves us so.
The Christ that dwells within us
Is the Greatest Power we know.
He will fight beside us;
Though the enemy is great
Who can stand against us,
He's the Captain of our fate.
Then we will conquer never fear,
So let the battle rage.
He has promised to be near, until
the end of the age.
We are more than conquerors through
Him that loves us so,
The Christ that dwells within us
Is the Greatest Power we know!

The Christ who dwells within you ... He is the key to "sanctification," to having power to live the Christian life. Believe Christ, trust Him, walk with Him in the Spirit, respond to His love with your own ... This is the difference between being a Christian and settling for "being religious."

For further thought

1. Memorize Rom. 8:28, then write out the verse in *Living Letters* paraphrase by listing after "all that happens" your problems, set backs, and defeats. Next write Rom. 8:28 again, listing after "all that happens" your victories, accomplishments, and progress.

2. Read Rom. 8:28-30 in several versions and translations. Do you feel called according to God's purpose? What is God's purpose for you? Compare I Peter 1:2, 20; Eph. 1:5, 11.

3. Compare Rom. 8:37-39 with I Cor. 15:54-58. Then write a brief statement, "Overwhelming victory is mine through Jesus Christ because":

CHAPTER 8

Who can know the mind of God?

At this point in his letter to Rome, Paul inserts what some call a "parenthesis." He stops to talk about "the fly in the ointment" as far as he is concerned: the rejection of God's plan of salvation in Christ by his own kinsmen—the Jews. Paul knows that God is bound to the Jews by solemn covenants. Are these just paper promises? Has God gone back on His word by offering salvation to the Gentiles? Is God capricious? Or is there a flaw in His plan? Read chapters 9-11 carefully. You will see that this parenthesis is, in another sense, a major girder in building a bridge to understanding the vital differences between Christianity—a trusting response to a sovereign God who reaches down to man, and religion—man reaching up to please or promote a god he has made himself ...

1-3Oh, Israel, my people! Oh, my Jewish brothers! How I long for you to come to Christ. My heart is heavy within me and I grieve bitterly day and night because of you. Christ knows and the Holy Spirit knows that it is no mere pretense when I say that I would be willing to be forever damned if that would save you.

4God has given you so much, but still you will not listen to Him. He took you as His own special, chosen people and led you along with a bright cloud of glory and told you how very much He wanted to bless you. He gave you His rules for daily life so you would know what He wanted you to do. He let you work for Him in the temple. He gave you mighty promises. 5Great men of God were your fathers, and Christ Himself was One of you, a Jew so far as His human nature is concerned, He Who now rules over all things and is blessed of God forever.

6Well then, did God's promises to His Jewish people become worthless when they refused to come to be saved?

Of course not.

For His promises are only to those who come. Only they are truly His people. They alone are truly Jews. So you see, not everyone born into a Jewish family is truly a Jew. 7Just because they come from Abraham doesn't make them truly Abraham's children. For the Scriptures say that the promises apply only to Abraham's son Isaac and Isaac's descendants, though Abraham had other children too. 8This means that not all of Abraham's children are children of God, but only the ones born as a result of God's special promise to Abraham.

[9]For God had promised, "Next year I will give you and Sarah a son (Isaac)."

[10-13]And years later, when Isaac was grown up and married, and Rebecca his wife was about to bear him twin children, God told her that Esau, the child born first, would be a servant to Jacob, his twin brother. In the words of the Scripture, "I chose to bless Jacob, but not Esau." And God said this before the children were even born, before they had done anything either good or bad. This proves that God was doing what He had decided from the beginning; it was not because of what the children did but because of what God wanted and chose.

[14]Was God being unfair?

Of course not. [15]For God had said to Moses, "If I want to be kind to someone, I will. And I will take pity on anyone I want to." [16]And so God's blessings are not given just because someone decides to have them or works hard to get them. They are given to those God wants to give them to. [17]Pharaoh king of Egypt was an example of this fact. For God told him He had given him the kingdom of Egypt for the very purpose of displaying the awesome power of God against him: so that all the world would hear about God's glorious name.

[18]So you see, God is kind to some just because He wants to be, and He makes some refuse to listen. [19]Well then, why does God blame them for not listening? Haven't they done what He made them do? [20]No, don't say that. Who are you to criticize God? Should the thing made say to the One who made it, "Why have you made me like this?" [21]When a man makes a jar out of clay, doesn't he have a right to use the same lump of clay to make one jar beautiful, to be used for holding flowers, and another to throw garbage into?

22And so God has a perfect right to be patient with whomever He wants to, even with those who are fit only for destruction; later on He will show His fury and power against them.

23-24And He has a right to take others such as ourselves, who have been made for pouring His glory into, whether we are Jews or Gentiles, and to be kind to us so that everyone can see how very great His glory is.

25Remember what it says in the book of Hosea? There God says that He will find other children for Himself (who are not from His Jewish family) and will love them, though no one had ever loved them before. 26And the heathen of whom it once was said, "You are not my people" shall be called "sons of the Living God." 27Isaiah the prophet cried out concerning the Jews that though there would be millions† of them, only a small number would ever be saved. 28For the Lord will execute His sentence upon the earth, quickly ending His dealings, justly cutting them short. 29And Isaiah says in another place that except for God's mercy all the Jews would be destroyed—all of them—just as everyone in the cities of Sodom and Gomorrah perished.

30Well then, what shall we say about these things? Just this, that God has given the Gentiles the opportunity to be saved by faith, even though they really were not seeking God. 31But the Jews, who tried so hard to be right with God by keeping His laws, did not find His salvation. 32Why not? Because they were trying to be saved by keeping the law and being good instead of by depending on faith. They have stumbled over the great stumbling-stone.

---

†literally: "as the sand of the sea," i.e., numberless.

[33]God warned them of this in the Scriptures when He said, "I have put a Rock in the path of the Jews, and many will stumble over Him (Jesus). But those who believe in Him will never be disappointed."

Who's in charge here?

God is not on trial. He runs the world according to His will. He is sovereign. We are His creation. Therefore, we have no business judging our Creator. We are not to be critics of God. He is our Critic. We are not to put God on trial. He alone is the supreme Judge. Each one of us must stand his own trial.

But it is not only because of God's wrath that He turns down an Esau or a Pharaoh and then turns around to have mercy on His chosen people. God knew before Esau was born how he would act, what he would do. On the basis of such careless behavior by Esau, God rejected him. Pharaoh was rejected not because God decided to be mean, but because Pharaoh refused to acknowledge the Lord. Pharaoh hardened his heart against God's miraculous revelation.

The problem is never with a holy God but with sinful man.

Questions will always persist. Our knowledge is limited since we are only created beings and not the Creator. Since God is loving and merciful (and we are confident of this because of Jesus Christ!), the miracle is not that God rejects sinful men, but that He is merciful to those who scarcely deserve it. The miracle is that He has not yet destroyed the world.

But what has this to do with the Jews and their rejection of Christ? Everything. Paul has news for them. God does not save entire nations. He saves individuals and whoever wants to may come ...

Romans 10:1-21

1Dear brothers, the longing of my heart and my prayer is that the Jewish people might be saved.

2I know what enthusiasm you have for the honor of God, but it is misdirected zeal. 3For you don't understand that Christ has died to make you right with God. Instead you are trying to make yourselves good enough to gain God's favor by keeping the Jewish laws and customs. But that is not God's way of salvation. 4You don't understand that Christ gives to those who trust in Him everything you are trying to get by keeping His laws. 5For as Moses said, if a person could be perfectly good and hold out against temptation all his life and never sin once, only then could he be saved.

6But the salvation that comes through faith says, "You don't need to search the heavens to find Christ and bring Him down to help you," and, 7"You don't need to go among the dead to bring Christ back to life again," 8for salvation that comes from trusting Christ—which is what we preach—is already within easy reach of each of us; in fact, it is as near as our own hearts and mouths. 9For if you tell others with your own mouth that Jesus Christ is your Lord, and believe in your own heart that God has raised Him from the dead, you will be saved. 10For it is by believing in his heart that a man becomes right with God; and with his mouth he tells others of his faith, confirming his salvation. 11For the Scriptures tell us that no one who believes in

Christ will ever be disappointed. 12Jew and Gentile are the same in this respect: they all have the same Lord Who generously gives His riches to all those who ask Him for them.

13Anyone who calls upon the name of the Lord will be saved.

14But how shall they ask Him to save them unless they believe in Him? And how can they believe in Him if they have never heard about Him? And how can they hear about Him unless someone tells them? 15And how will anyone go and tell them unless someone sends him? That is what the Scriptures are talking about when they say, "How beautiful are the feet of those who preach the Gospel of peace, and bring glad tidings of good things." In other words, how welcome are those who come preaching God's Good News! 16But not everyone who hears the Good News has welcomed it, for Isaiah the prophet said, "Lord, who has believed me when I told them?" 17Yet faith comes from listening to this Good News—the Good News about Christ, Who is the Word of God.

18But what about the Jews? Have they heard God's word?

Yes, for it has gone wherever they are. The Good News has been told to the ends of the earth.

19And did they know that God would give His salvation to others if they refused to take it?

Yes, for even back in the time of Moses, God had said that He would make His people jealous and try to wake them up by giving His salvation to the foolish heathen nations. 20And later on Isaiah said boldly that God would be found by people who weren't even looking for Him, and they would be saved.

²¹In the meantime, He keeps on reaching out His hands to the Jews but they keep arguing and refusing to come.

Living by the law: a dead-end street

Paul makes one thing clear in this passage. Religious zeal is not enough.

The Jews thought they could make themselves right with God with meticulous obedience to the laws and observance of customs. There are many striking examples and anecdotes about the lengths Jews would go to obey the law.

For example, the Fourth Book of Maccabees (part of the Apocrypha) tells of how Eleazar, a Jewish priest, was brought before Antiochus Epiphanes a Syrian King who was determined to stamp out the Jewish religion. Eleazar was ordered to eat pork. In strict adherence to Jewish laws, he refused. Antiochus ordered the old man to be beaten with whips and he was soon a bloody mass. The cruel Syrian soldiers finally took pity and brought him meat that was not pork, saying to eat it and say it was. Eleazar refused and finally was killed. As he died, he prayed, "I am dying by fiery torments for thy Law's sake." Eleazar resisted to the death *for the law's sake*. He died for a law that forbade him to eat pork! A rather pointless death, you say? Not to Eleazar, not to the Jew who believed that living by the law was the way to God.

But Paul informs his kinsmen of the truth that was revealed to him on the Damascus Road: You don't have to reach up to God by trying to keep His laws (vs. 4-7). You simply respond to God as He reaches down to you. You believe (in your heart, not just your head) that Jesus is Lord and confess (with your mouth) that He is your Saviour from sin. And—Jew or Gentile—God accepts you.

One more point ... Paul reminds the Jews that God's plan never was limited to one nation (vs. 19, 20). The prophets spoke long ago of how God would be found by people *who weren't even looking for Him.*

But where does this leave the Jews? What does it mean to be one of God's chosen nation? Here is Paul's conclusion ...

Romans 11:1-33

¹I ask then, has God rejected and deserted His people the Jews?

Oh no, not at all. Remember that I myself am a Jew, a descendant of Abraham and a member of Benjamin's family. ²⁻³No, God has not discarded His own people whom He chose from the very beginning. Do you remember what the Scriptures say about this? Elijah the prophet was complaining to God about the Jews, telling God how they had killed the prophets and torn down God's altars; Elijah claimed that he was the only one left in all the land who still loved God, and now they were trying to kill him too. ⁴And do you remember how God replied? God said, "No, you are not the only one left. I have seven thousand others besides you who still love Me and have not bowed down to idols!"

⁵It is the same today.

Not all the Jews have turned away from God. There are a few being saved as a result of God's

84

kindness in choosing them. 6And if it is by God's kindness, then it is not by their being good enough. For in that case the free gift would no longer be free —it isn't free when it is earned.

7So this is the situation: most of the Jews have not found the favor of God they are looking for. A few have, the ones God has picked out, but the eyes of the others have been blinded. 8This is what our Scriptures refer to when they say that God has put them to sleep, shutting their eyes and ears so that they do not understand what we are talking about when we tell them of Christ. And so it is to this very day. 9King David spoke of this same thing when he said, "Let their good food and other blessings trap them into thinking all is well between themselves and God. Let these good things boomerang upon them and fall back upon their heads to justly crush them. 10Let their eyes be dim, so that they cannot see, and let them walk bent-backed forever with a heavy load."

11Did God make His Jewish people stumble like this for the purpose of bringing disaster to them? Oh no, His purpose was to make His salvation available to the Gentiles, and then the Jews would be jealous and begin to want God's salvation for themselves.

12Now if the whole world became rich as a result of God's offer of salvation, when the Jews stumbled over it and turned it down, think how much greater a blessing the world will share in later on when the Jews too come to Christ.

13As you know, God has appointed me as a special messenger to you Gentiles. I lay great stress on this and remind the Jews about it as often as I can, 14so that if possible I can make them want what you Gentiles have and in that way save some of them. [15]And how wonderful it is when they become Christians. When God turned away from them it meant that He turned to the rest of the world to offer His salvation; and now it is even more wonderful when some of the Jews come to Christ. It is like dead people coming back to life again.

[16]And since Abraham and the prophets are God's people, their children will be too. For if the roots of the tree are holy, the branches will be too. [17]But some of these branches from Abraham's tree, some of the Jews, have been broken off. And you Gentiles who were branches from, we might say, a wild olive tree, were grafted in. So now you too receive the blessing God has promised Abraham and his children, sharing in God's rich nourishment of His own special olive tree. [18]But you must be careful not to brag about being put in to replace the branches that were broken off. Remember that you are important only because you are now a part of God's tree; you are just a branch, not a root. [19]"Well," you may be saying, "those branches were broken off to make room for me so I must be pretty good." [20]Watch out! Remember that those branches, the Jews, were broken off because they didn't believe God, and you are there only because you do. Do not be proud; be humble and grateful—and careful. [21]For if God did not spare the branches He put there in the first place, He won't spare you either.

[22]See how God is both so kind and so severe. He is very hard on those who disobey, but very good to you if you continue to love and trust Him. But if you don't, you too will be cut off. [23]On the other hand, if the Jews leave their unbelief behind them and come back to God, God will graft them back into the tree again. He has the power to do it. [24]For if God was willing to take you who were so far away

from Him—being part of a wild olive tree—and graft you into His own good tree—a very unusual thing to do—don't you see that He will be far more ready to put the Jews back again, who were there in the first place?

25I want you to know about this mystery, dear brothers, so that you will not feel proud and start bragging. Yes, it is true that most of the Jews have set themselves against the Gospel now, but this will last only until all of you Gentiles have come to Christ—those of you who will. 26And then all Israel will be saved. Do you remember what the prophets said about this? "There shall come out of Zion a Deliverer, and He shall turn the Jews from all ungodliness. 27At that time I will take away their sins, just as I promised."

28Now most of the Jews are enemies of the Gospel. They hate it. But this has been a benefit to you, for it has resulted in God giving His gifts to you Gentiles. But the Jews are still beloved of God because of His promises to Abraham, Isaac, and Jacob. 29For God's gifts and His call can never be withdrawn; He will never go back on His promises. 30Once you were rebels against God, but when the Jews refused His gifts God was merciful to you instead. 31And now the Jews are the rebels, but some day they will share in God's mercy upon you. 32For God arranged that all be sinners so that He could have mercy upon all alike.

33Oh what a wonderful God we have! How great are His wisdom and knowledge and riches. How impossible it is for us to understand His decisions and His methods.

No salvation in 'The Establishment'

In the first verses of chapter 11, Paul repeats what he said in chapter 9. God does not save nations; He saves individuals. The correct question is not: "Has God discarded His people, the Jews?" The correct question is: "Which Jews are responding to God's gift of salvation in Christ?" It was precisely on this point that the Jews made a fatal error. They forgot that from the start God's terms were personal responsibility and individual faith. The Jews started thinking that they had salvation because of being members of a special nation. They became, in a way, "organization men." They used the law to promote their own version of "The Establishment."

And so God cut many of them off, "broke them off," if you want to use the term in Paul's illustration of the olive tree (vs. 16-24). And Paul warns the Gentiles to not start feeling smug. They are grafted into the olive tree for one reason: their faith. This is God's plan right now, but He has not forgotten His covenants with the Jews. Even though most of them are now enemies of the gospel, there will come a day when they will be saved through God's mercy.

Hard to grasp? Yes, it is. It is enough to convince you that no man can know or completely understand the mind of God ...

Romans 11:34-36

34For who among us can know the mind of the Lord? Who knows enough to be His counselor and guide? 35And who has ever given anything to the Lord first as payment for something in return? 36For everything comes from God alone. Everything lives by His power, and everything is for His glory.

To him be glory evermore.

Could you trust a God who wasn't in charge?

If God does not rule, then all other belief in God matters very little. If God is not sovereign, we cannot trust Him after all. How can you trust a God who is not in charge?

The Lord is King. He is to be worshiped, not used. He is to be adored, not merely made attractive. His wisdom is beyond us. He makes His own decisions without asking for our poor opinions.

We can do little else but acknowledge that God is God. At the end of this probing section in which Paul has tried to find out answers to some real questions, he can only fall on his knees in wonder and praise of God. He is overwhelmed at the wisdom which lies beyond him. He can only worship. God, in Christ, is a Person, not a religion.

There is a famous statue of Christ in Brazil. But the face of Jesus is so turned that the only way to look into His eyes is to get down on your knees and look up.

That is the only way to see God, too—in humility and faith. This is how to be a Christian without being religious.

For further thought

1. God's sovereignty and man's freedom are a paradox that is hard to understand. But if God were not sovereign, what kind of a God would He be? And if man were not free to choose or reject God, what would man be?

2. Compare Rom. 11:33-36 with Rom. 8:28-39. Write down some ways they tie together.

CHAPTER 9

Is it God's will?

All Christians ask this question. Some ask sincerely, with real concern. Some are curious. Some are worried, even afraid. Some ask too late, after they have gone ahead with ill-fated plans. Some try "formulas" like "Read a chapter a day and pray." Others see God's will as a sort of career computer— a "master plan" that guarantees you the right job. Whatever the motive, whatever the means for finding an answer, the question of God's will dogs the Christian's steps with "unhurrying chase and unperturbed pace."* But instead of playing religious roulette with formulas and master plans, perhaps we should first ask if being in God's will is a Christian's destination or a way of traveling. Paul knew the road well . . .

---

*From the "Hound of Heaven," by Francis Thompson.

1And so, dear brothers, I plead with you to give your bodies to God. Let them be a living sacrifice, holy—the kind He can accept. When you think of what He has done for you, is this too much to ask?

2Don't copy the fashions and customs of this world, but be a new and different person with a fresh newness in all you do and think. Then you will see from your own experience how His ways will really satisfy you.

Do you have your cart ahead of your horse?

Romans 12:1 . . . used frequently in memory verse lists . . . often the text for the speaker's closing challenge at a Christian camp or conference . . . but also the hinge on which the Book of Romans turns to take a new tack.

For 11 chapters Paul has dealt with what a Christian believes and why. He has told you how to know Christ and be saved from the penalty of sin. He has told you how to be empowered by Christ and be freed from the power of sin. Now, with the start of chapter 12, he begins telling you how to serve Christ—in effect, how to find and do God's will.

Alan Redpath has described God's will as two-fold. The will of God concerning character is *universal*, but the will of God concerning service is *individual*.* All right, you'll probably buy that. It's easy to see that God wants you to develop in Christian character. But the service angle—just

---

*From *Getting to Know the Will of God* by Alan Redpath, p. 1. Copyright © 1954. Inter-Varsity Press. Used by permission.

**STEP ONE IN FINDING GOD'S WILL:
PRESENT YOUR BODY AS A LIVING SACRIFICE**

what you should do, when and how to do it—this is
the stickler; so what good does it do to know that
God's will has two parts?

Just this. A lot of Christians put the cart before
the horse. They fume and fret about what God
wants them to do (service) when they are spiritually unprepared to do it (character). Here is where
Rom. 12:1 comes in. Before God wants your service,
He wants a guarantee that He really has *you*. Paul
doesn't mince words. We are to give our bodies as a
living sacrifice.

Sounds almost primitive, doesn't it? How personal
can Paul get? After all, it's not too hard to sit in
church and promise God your soul and your spirit.
After all, these are proper things for God to have—
they are His responsibility with heaven and all that's
coming up some day. But our *bodies*? Really, this
relationship may be getting a bit too close for
comfort. This could cramp one's style, get in the
way, cause inhibitions. Why this sort of thing could
lead to being more than religious!

Exactly.

God didn't just save your soul. He saved *you*—your total self, and this includes your body. When a Christian gets serious enough about Christ to commit his body—what he does with hands, eyes, ears, mouth, etc.—to God, then he is ready to know and do God's will.

Too much to ask? Perhaps, but before you protest, think, says Paul, of what Christ did for you.

So the first step is God's will for your character. And you cannot fulfill God's purpose for your character until you present your body—your total you—to God in an intelligent, determined act of dedication and commitment. You don't do this once a year—at camp or during the annual evangelistic crusade. You do it daily. And as you give all of yourself to God, you put the horse where it belongs—in front of the cart. You are ready to move and act within God's will. The power you need (your Christian character) is where it can do some good (in Christian service).

WELL, WHEN YOU PUT IT THAT WAY . . .

DOES GOD ASK FOR TOO MUCH?
REMEMBER WHAT HE DID FOR YOU

All right, let's say you do all this. In which direction do you head? What about service, specifically *specific* service?

A good test of a lot of your plans and activities is right in Rom. 12:2: "Don't copy the fashions and customs of this world ..." or in J. B. Phillips' classic terms: "Don't let the world squeeze you into its own mold ..."

This is not to say that you're supposed to become some kind of oddball. But you are to steer clear of the world's superficial value system, which places a premium on sensuality, sex and sick humor. The Christian often faces some tough decisions on what is "worldly" and what is acceptable to God. A key checkpoint is your motive. As J. P. Morgan once said: "A man always has two reasons for doing anything—a 'good' reason and the real reason." The particular situation may be difficult but the choice is usually clear: are you trying to please yourself, the "in group," the crowd? Or are you interested in pleasing God?

"All very good," you say, "but the world is very real, and I am in it all day long. How do I resist the squeeze, stay out of the mold?" Rom. 12:2 goes on to suggest: "Be a new and different person with a fresh newness in all you do and think."

You think with your brain, so if you are interested in "thinking new," take inventory on what you are watching and reading. The "new morality" prophets preach from a bible called *Playboy* and parrot various versions of one tiresome text: "Eat, drink and make Mary, for tomorrow the finance company may repossess your Jaguar."

ORIGINAL OR A COPY?
ARE YOU

It would be interesting to know how many Christians outwardly claim they are interested in knowing God's will, yet they are hooked in one way or another by the continuous bombardment, in ads, TV and magazines, that is designed to increase the appetite for sex, things, pleasure. Not that there is anything wrong with sex, things, and pleasure. It's just that few of us really need stimulation of our appetites in these areas. There is plenty of appetite there already, and it's a case of learning how to control these natural drives and desires and bring them into line with the subject of this chapter—God's will.

But even policing your TV programs and censoring your subscriptions isn't the final answer. And Paul knew it, because he advises in Rom. 12:2 to "renew your mind from within."

The trap that snares a lot of Christians is the old dual standard; one set of rules for outward behavior, another standard for the mind—the "thought life." It's not hard to learn how to play the game called "churchianity." You learn to not do certain things (or at least not to get caught doing them). You learn to show up at church often enough to be labeled "active" or "faithful." You look pretty spiritual, and all the while your thought life is running "amuck in muck" or feasting on materialism, greed, hatred, jealousy, etc., etc.

So what do you do? If you want God's will, give Him your total self—a living sacrifice—and that means your body *and* your thoughts, your mind, which He can renew from within, if you let Him.

Perhaps by now you are getting the message: God's will is not something you order by mail. You don't use formulas, but there are checkpoints to apply to any situation. F. B. Meyer, a famous preacher of his day, was on a sea voyage. Coming into port one night, it was very stormy and the entrance to the harbor looked very narrow. Meyer turned to the captain on the bridge beside him and said, "Captain, how do you know when to make the turn into the harbor?"

"That's an art," said the captain. "Do you see those three lights on shore? When they're all in a straight line, I go right in."

Alan Redpath* applies this story to finding God's will by pointing out three "navigation lights" that are available to the Christian for guidance: 1. the Bible; 2. the inward witness of the Holy Spirit; 3. outward circumstances. When these three are in line, go on in. Until they are, try to wait. Waiting is hard, but often it can be the best thing to do.

*Ibid., p. 12.

Let's look at these three lights more closely. *The guidance of God's Word* is primary, basic. It's interesting to note that many of us say we are interested in God's will, but we balk at checking our plans and habits against the plain teaching of the Bible. How can you say you are seeking God's will, if you don't know what the Bible says? This is like going to someone for advice, but not letting him talk. You actually want him to agree with everything you say.

Another mistaken concept is to treat the Bible like an "answer book." You page through, trying to find "just the right verse" to help you out. The Bible is God's message, His conversation to you. If you are serious about communicating with God, start talking to Him—and let Him talk to you. This is the first step in walking in the Spirit. (See chapter 6 for a review.)

The witness of the Holy Spirit comes as you walk in the Spirit. Prayer is vital here. It's unfortunate that we have made "I'll have to pray about it" something of a cliche. Maybe we should change the phrase to "I will talk with God about it." With God, not at God. Some prayer lists sound like Christmas lists. Other's sound like assignments that God should carry out because we are "so spiritual, so deserving."

The inner witness of the Spirit is always available. It comes from walking and living in the Spirit, but this is a constant daily thing, not some button you push when you think you "need a little advice" from God.

Take a look at outward circumstances LAST. We

usually reverse the order. *First,* we call a committee meeting. *First,* we examine all the evidence. *First,* we talk it over with so and so or read up on the subject. But if you start with circumstances, you seldom get beyond them. How can you evaluate circumstances if you have no guidance from God's Word and God's Spirit?

But suppose you feel you have the Word and the Spirit lined up fairly well. How do you evaluate or act upon circumstances? This can be intriguing, exciting. For one thing you have to act in faith on what you already know. Is it evident that there are certain actions that would be worth taking? Some people call this "trying different doors." Sometimes God will slam shut every door but the one He wants you to walk through. You may have to try several doors to learn which is the right one.

No, God's will doesn't drop out of the blue in a special delivery letter. But He has written to you— in His Word. He will talk to you, with the inner witness of His Spirit. And He will guide you as you weigh outward circumstances.

Still sound like a formula? Well you can make it that. You can be "very religious" about these three checkpoints ... or you can use them like a Christian, in faith, trust, and commitment. Then you will see from your own experience how God's ways will really satisfy you.

For other practical pointers on finding God's will, read on in Romans 12 for some tips on how to take an honest look at yourself. Be sure, says Paul, that you see the plus as well as the minus side ...

Romans 12:3-8

[3] As God's messenger I give each of you God's warning: be honest in your estimate of yourselves, measuring your value by how much faith God has given you.

[4-5] For just as there are many parts to our bodies, so it is with Christ's body. We are all parts of it, and it takes every one of us to make it complete, for we each have different work to do. So we belong to each other, and each needs all the others. [6] God has given each of us the ability to do certain things well. So if God has given you the ability to prophesy, then prophesy whenever you can—as often as your faith is strong enough to produce a message from God.

[7] If your gift is that of serving others, serve them well. Teachers should do a good job of teaching. [8] The preacher should see to it that his sermons are strong and helpful. If God has given you money, be generous in helping others with it. If God has given you administrative ability and put you in charge of the work of others, take the responsibility seriously. And if yours is the gift of kindness to others, do it cheerfully.

Only one thing really counts

Be *honest in your estimate*, says Paul. Some Christians have a tendency to think they are "no good," always failing, never really accomplishing anything. If you're in this boat, abandon ship right now. God has accepted you. You are a person of worth. Christ died for you. You have potential. Don't sell yourself—or the Lord Jesus Christ—short.

The other side of the honesty coin is for those with the superiority complex. None of us is humanity's gift to God. In fact God had to send *us* a gift

99

so we could get out of the human snake pit called sin.

As usual, Paul zeroes in on the needful thing: faith. Your *faith* is what matters, not your GPA, SAT score, or the number of horses under your hood. Your *faith* is what counts, not the fact that you were once voted Mr. Wonderful or Miss Personality.

All Christians need each other and we all need Christ. There is work to do—serving, teaching, preaching, making (and *giving*) money, just plain being kind to others. And, as you will see in the next chapter, Paul has some explicit words on how to get on with it ...

For further thought

1. Memorize Rom. 12:1 and study it in several translations. Compare Matt. 16:24 and Luke 9:23. What does self-denial mean to you? What does self-denial have to do with Rom. 12:1?

2. Read Rom. 12:2 in several translations, especially *Phillips*. Compare these vs. on resisting worldliness: I Cor. 7:31; Gal. 6:14; II Tim. 2:4; Heb. 11:24,25; I John 2:15. Write a definition of "worldliness" and three practical ways to avoid being worldly.

3. Analyze the way you are seeking God's will. Is the "cart" (your service to God) before the "horse" (your Christian character)? How are you using the three guidelines for finding God's will that this chapter mentions? (1. God's Word; 2. the Spirit's witness; 3. circumstances)

4. List negative ways (don'ts) and positive ways (do's) in which you are renewing your mind from within.

CHAPTER 10

Is your Christianity really...
COUNTERFEIT LOVE?

Counterfeit love for Christ? Counterfeit Christianity? Not mine! I'll have you know that I'm born again ... washed in the blood of the lamb. None of this Mickey Mouse liberalism for me. I *know* I'm on my way to heaven. I've got my doctrine straight, and that's for sure. I serve the Lord, I even tithe (sometimes). I give my old clothes to missions. I put Scripture references in all my Christmas cards. I, I ...

But one thing more is needful ...

[9]Don't just pretend that you love others: really love them. Hate what is wrong. Stand on the side of the good. [10]Love each other with brotherly affection and delight to honor each other.

[11]Never be lazy in your work but serve the Lord enthusiastically.

[12]Be glad for all God is planning for you. Be patient in trouble, and prayerful always.

[13]When God's children are in need, you be the one to help them out. And get into the habit of inviting guests home for dinner; or, if they need lodging, for the night.

[14]If someone harms you, don't curse him; pray that God will bless him.

[15]When others are happy, be happy with them. If they are sad, share their sorrow.

[16]Work happily together. Don't try to act big. Don't try to get into the good graces of important people, but enjoy the company of ordinary folks. And don't think you know it all!

[17]Never pay back evil for evil. Do things in such a way that everyone can see you are honest clear through.

[18]Don't quarrel with anyone. Be at peace with everyone, just as much as you possibly can. [19]Dear friends, never avenge yourselves. Let anger cool, for God has said that He will pay back those deserving it. [20]So feed your enemy if he is hungry. If he is thirsty give him something to drink and you will be "heaping coals of fire on his head." In other words, he will feel ashamed of himself for what he has done to you. [21]Don't let evil get the upper hand but conquer evil by doing good.

Can you quit playing 'Let's Pretend'?

Conquer evil by doing good. Paul spent a lot of time at the beginning of his letter to Rome on the need for believing what is good. Now he is getting down where we live. In fact, he is starting to sound like a meddler. He wants us to *do* what is good.

Christians speak much of loving God, loving one another, loving mankind. What does all this "lovely" talk mean? For one thing, says Paul, it means that you quit playing "let's pretend." Quit being a phony.

For example, Paul says we should "Hate what is wrong. Stand on the side of the good" (v. 9). This means more than just staying out of trouble. It means getting involved with trying to change things for the better—where you work, around your school and above all, in your own home with your own family.

One of the major traps for the Christian today is that he is surrounded by so much evil and sin that he grows used to it. He is no longer shocked. He learns to "get along," to keep his mouth shut, to not make trouble. A lot of Christians avoid evil, but *they do not hate it*. A lot of Christians are for the good, but *they do not fight for it*. A lot of what is called Christianity is really passive compromise with sin.

But where do you get the power, the motivation to conquer evil by doing good? Love. Genuine love is the needed thing. "Don't just pretend that you love others: really love them" (v. 9). Romans 12 is a short course in being concerned for others rather than yourself. This is the hardest thing we can be asked to do. Our psychological make-up demands that we worry first about Old No. 1. Self-preservation is as natural as breathing. We are quick to defend ourselves and our rights. Our egos are labeled "handle with care." We bruise easily.

And then we become Christians. Suddenly we have no rights, only duties. How unfair can things get? Yes, it would be unfair if the Christian had no resources, no help. To live as Paul suggests in Romans 12 is humanly impossible. It is, however, *supernaturally* possible, as he clearly pointed out back in chapters 6, 7 and 8 of Romans. Walking in the Spirit is not some quaint religious exercise. It is for the street, where *you* live.

Paul is getting painfully practical now. You say you are crucified with Christ? You say you have "died to sin and risen again with Christ?" What better way, then, to test all your new powers than to see if you actually can live and love unselfishly. To try to love others unselfishly and at the same time be concerned with standing up for your rights is a contradiction in terms. You cannot serve God and self. You cannot go around with the Bible in one hand and waving your personal Bill of Rights in the other.

"But so few Christians around my church really show unselfish love. Why should I be the one to start?"

Yes, why should you? You probably wouldn't do a very good job of it anyway. People would just think you had suddenly gone a little hyperspiritual

YOU CANNOT SERVE GOD AND SELF. YOU CANNOT GO AROUND WITH THE BIBLE IN ONE HAND AND YOUR PERSONAL BILL OF RIGHTS IN THE OTHER . . .

or something. You could even lose some social prestige . . .

There are all kinds of excuses "to not get carried away" with the list of good deeds in Romans 12. But the excuses don't make the standard any less valid. Paul is not nailing up a list of laws that the Christian has to obey without a slip. He is setting up goals to aim at, to set your sights on.

Of course you won't do a perfect job of unselfish loving. Of course you may be criticized, even laughed at. But when Paul talks in Romans 12 of honoring others, of never being lax in Christian zeal, of being glad and patient in trouble, of helping others in need, of praying for those who harm you . . . he is simply putting muscle on the idea of presenting your body as a "living sacrifice" (Rom. 12:1).

This business of being a living sacrifice was well put by a missionary who had this advice for a young fellow who was thinking about the mission field:

"Instead of going to the refrigerator for a bite before going to bed, or to the corner drugstore for a coke, try going to bed without it. You won't die and you won't miss it when you can't get it out here.

"Try cutting the chatter in order to get home earlier or to give more time to studies or devotions. Out here you may have to go for months at a time without friendly chinfests with others of your own language. Discipline yourself to eat things you don't like, without choking and without griping.

"Kick yourself out of bed before the heat comes on in order to spend time with the Lord. Next camp you go to, try sleeping for two weeks on the floor. Find out if your call and Christian joy vary in inverse proportion to the comforts and conveniences.

"I'm not dreaming these things up. I'm thinking of people who so missed ice cream and candy, who couldn't get along without the fellowship of others, who were always complaining of the cold, or who couldn't settle down to serious work unless they had eight hours on an inner spring mattress, that they made excuses for not getting the work done. In some cases these were definitely contributing factors to their leaving the field, quitting."*

"But I'm not going to the mission field," you say. Aren't you? Where do you think you are right now? Is your home, or school, or place of work really any less a mission field than the streets of Bombay or the Auca country of Ecuador?

Every Christian is a missionary, because a missionary is one who is sent to bring and *to be* the Good News to others. Every Christian is called to present his body as a living sacrifice. Don't just pretend to love others. Really love them—by going out of your way to help them, by taking their guff, by overlooking their faults, by refusing to retaliate,

---

*Wycliffe Bible Translators. Used by permission.

106

especially in the sophisticated game of repartee and cutting conversation that so many of us play so well.

Does your Christianity reveal a bogus brand of counterfeit love? Genuine Christian love means first that you sincerely, unselfishly offer your daily life to God. He then proves, tests, and tempers your sincerity and unselfishness by sending you out to live among your fellow men.

We all fail, some of us many times, to show perfect Christian love. But faith begins where failure leaves off. We are not only saved from the penalty of sin by faith. We not only conquer sin and temptation by faith. *We serve and love by faith as well.*

It is in this living and loving and serving . . . it is in the daily routine—the "rat race" of life—that you have countless opportunities to be a living sacrifice . . . or just a burnt offering.

For further thought

1. Memorize Rom. 12:9 in *Living Letters* paraphrase. Compare with Rom. 12:1,2. What is the necessary foundation for genuine Christian love?

2. Some non-Christians seem to show more love for others than a lot of Christians do. Why is this so?

3. It is easy to complain that it seems impossible to love certain individuals because they are so obnoxious, so unlovable. There are people we just don't like. Read Rom. 12:9-21 carefully. How many of Paul's suggestions for loving others depend on how well we like them? What is the difference between liking someone and showing him love by your actions?

CHAPTER 11

The only law you need

"Only one law to obey? Now that wouldn't be so bad. If there's anything that I'm fed up with it's rules, rules, rules, Regulations. Codes. Curfews. Red tape. Please fill out this form. Please sign your name on all three copies. Traffic laws, tax laws, draft laws. I'm being strangled by authoritarian bureaucracy. One of these days I'll show them. I'm fed up with their overbearing bungling. It's certainly true that the government that governs least governs best. The leaster the better for my money . . ."

Hold on, friend. So you are fed up with this idea of authority, especially the unfairness, the corruption, the unconcerned inefficiency. You want to hear the hammer of justice, the bell of freedom. But first take a look at that "only law you need." Paul's views on authorities and governments may surprise you ...

Romans 13:1-10

1Obey the government, for God is the One who has put it there. There is no government anywhere that God has not placed in power. 2So those who refuse to obey the laws of the land are refusing to obey God, and punishment will follow. 3For the policeman is not there to frighten people doing right; but those doing evil will always fear him. So if you don't want to be afraid, keep the laws and you will get along well. 4The policeman is sent by God to help you. But if you are doing something wrong, of course you should be afraid, for he will have you punished. He is sent by God for that very purpose. 5So you must obey the laws for two reasons: to keep from being punished and because you know you should.

6Pay your taxes too, for these same two reasons. For government workers need to be paid so that they can keep on doing God's work, serving you. 7Pay everyone whatever he ought to have: pay your taxes and import duties gladly, obey those over you and give honor and respect to all those to whom it is due.

8Pay all your debts except the debt of love for others; never finish paying that! For if you love them, you will be obeying all of God's laws, fulfilling all His requirements. 9If you love your neighbor as much as you love yourself you will not want to harm or cheat

him, or kill him or steal from him. And you won't sin
with his wife or want what is his, or do anything else
the Ten Commandments say are wrong. All ten are
wrapped up in this one, to love your neighbor as you
love yourself. [10]Love does no wrong to anyone. That's
why it fully satisfies all of God's requirements. It is the
only law you need.

Are you behind in your debts?

Love is the only law you need. Here we are back
to love again. But what a strange combination—
government and love. What does love have to do
with paying taxes or staying within the speed limit?

Everything.

Paul doesn't insert these thoughts on obeying
civil government because he simply wants to fill
space.

In chapter 12 Paul talks about living the Christian life in the daily routine, the daily contacts we
make with others. It was only natural then that
Paul would expand his thinking past the "one to
one" situations of Romans 12 and comment on
living the Christian life as a member of a community, as a citizen of a government.

Wherever there are men, there is government of
some kind. And Paul makes one thing crystal clear
right at the start: *all governments are in power
because God has allowed them to be.*

This means that all governments—even cruel,
despotic dictatorships—are part of God's plan and
permissive will. Tyrants carry out his purposes
along with saints.

When Paul wrote his letter to the church at

Rome, the terrible persecutions and martyrdoms of Christians were still a few years away. They would come soon enough in A.D. 64 when Nero needed a scapegoat to explain a terrible fire that leveled most of Rome. Christians were prime suspects for any kind of crime because of their disobedience of Roman law, which demanded that citizens have "no god above Caesar." But Christians *did* have a God above Caesar: the Lord Jesus Christ. They refused to offer sacrifices before statues of the emperor. They worshiped none of the pagan deities or idols which were seen everywhere in Rome. Ironically, their strange beliefs won for Christians the title of "atheist" because, as far as the typical solid Roman citizens were concerned, they did not believe in the gods.

Although a Jew, Paul was born a Roman citizen. He knew Roman law and the tensions that a Christian believer would have when living under Roman rule. And so Paul had reasons for including a few words on the Christian concept of citizenship.

For one thing *Paul did not want Christians to be labeled as being as rebellious as the Jews*. Palestine was probably Rome's biggest headache. None of the Jews were content under Roman rule. There was even a band of fanatical Jewish "guerrilla fighters" called Zealots who were pledged to carry on constant terrorism. They would not only cut Roman throats when they could, but they would burn the crops and homes of fellow Jews who paid tribute to the Roman government. Paul wanted no part of this kind of Jewish insurrection. It would be a direct contradiction of Christian faith and ethics.

How could a Christian witness of his love for Christ and love for others while cutting someone's throat?

Paul had still more reasons for his teachings on obeying the civil powers. And they apply just as readily today as they did then. For example, *Paul knew that no man can completely disassociate himself from his community.* Being a member of a society brings responsibilities as well as privileges. A man has duties to his nation as well as to his church, even if he does not agree with everything the government stands for or does. Controversy over governments—what kind, how much, how little—has raged since time began. But there is little doubt about the necessity of government. Without the organization and protection of the state, we would all be forced to live by the law of the jungle —survival of the strong and the vicious.

In addition the state provides services and advantages that men could not possibly enjoy individually: water supply, sewage, the courts, schools. No one is free to take everything he can from the state and not give back his cooperation and loyalty.

But perhaps Paul's most important reason for advising support of the Roman government was because *he saw Rome as God's tool for keeping the lid on an otherwise hopelessly explosive situation.*

Paul believed in using the "pax Romana" (the Roman peace that prevailed during his time) to the advantage of the gospel. As long as there was peace, even a rigidly (sometimes cruelly) enforced one, Paul saw greater opportunity to spread the gospel. Whether Rome knew it or not, in Paul's mind Rome was helping him do his missionary

WITHOUT GOVERNMENT, WE WOULD BE FORCED
TO LIVE BY THE LAW OF THE JUNGLE...

work. And for this reason, the wise Christian would always try to help, not hinder the state.*

And so Paul gives a brief refresher course on good citizenship: obey the laws of the land, respect and cooperate with the police (if you're innocent, why worry?). Obey the law to keep from being punished and also because you know it's the thing you should do. Pay your taxes and fees; obey those in authority; and give honor and respect to high offices (vs. 1-7).

With v. 8 notice how Paul makes one of his

---

*See *The Letter to the Romans*, William Barclay. Westminster Press. Used by permission.

typically fluid shifts into theological overdrive. "Pay all your debts except the debt of love for others; never finish paying that!" What an odd jump in thought, from prosaic things like policemen, taxes and honoring authorities to the "debt of love." What does Paul mean?

Simply this. Pay your debts—the money you owe the grocer, the department store, the used car lot. Go along with authority wherever you find it: in the corridors of the school, on the streets of the city, in the aisles and hallways at work. Oil the wheels of social justice. Keep society running as smoothly as possible. Don't offend or violate the rights of others ... but ... *if you really want motivation and power to be a good citizen, never stop paying your debt of love to all men.*

And what is this debt of love? To love your neighbor as yourself. Keep this command, this law, and you automatically keep all the others. If you are really concerned with keeping the law of love, it is the only law you really need. Then civil laws are not problems or objects of protests and demonstrations. Civil laws are only guidelines to help you achieve your aim: loving ot ers as you love yourself and thereby fulfilling all of God's requirements.

Most laws, whether biblical, civil or even those laid down in a family, are groups of "thou shalt nots." Laws and rules—at home, at school, at work, in cities, states and countries—are laid down to prevent the rights of others from being trampled. Laws and rules are necessary to run a society composed of men who are under the universal curse of sin. Love is the only law we need, but few of us try or even want to obey it.

What Paul is saying in Romans 13 is that Christians have a distinct responsibility as well as a definite advantage in the area of good citizenship. The Christian citizen's first question is not: "What are my rights? Am I getting justice?" His first concern is: "Am I living by the law of love?"

By concerning yourself with the positive "do's" of love, you automatically avoid entanglement with a long list of "don'ts" that is necessary to insure justice for all. Obeying the law of love throws a completely different light on good citizenship. You obey institutional rules and regulations not because you primarily want to avoid trouble, but because you seek the common good of all. You obey traffic laws not to stay out of jail or traffic court, but because you respect the lives and property of others. You pay your taxes and fees not because you fear a possible chat with IRS, but because you believe in government and financing its operation.

Applications of the law of love are endless. The Christian who obeys the law of love does not cheat or steal. He does not kill or cripple enemies, but tries to turn them into friends.

The Christian who lives by the law of love does not see authority as a threat. Nor does he see imperfections or even gross errors in government as reason to riot or demonstrate unlawfully. The Christian is not a bystander in his society. Actually he should be in the thick of the battle for justice, morality and the right. But the Christian operates with a different motive. He seeks justice for all, yes,

115

but justice is primarily a negative concept, based on avoiding or preventing the doing of wrongs to others. The law of love goes beyond justice. The law of love seeks the positive doing of good to others. It is the only law a Christian needs.

There are still other reasons for good citizenship. Paul closes chapter 13 with a note of realistic urgency, and the crisp language of *Living Letters* needs no comment, except to suggest that if a Christian is looking for a "life verse" he might consider Rom. 13:14:

Romans 13:11-14

11Another reason for right living is this: you know how late it is; time is running out. Wake up, for the coming of the Lord is nearer now than when we first believed. 12The night is far gone, the day of His return will soon be here. So we must quit the evil deeds of darkness and put on the armor of upright living. 13We must be honest and true so that all can see that everything we do is good. We are not to spend our time in wild parties and drunkenness, or in adultery and lust, or in fighting, or wishing for things that don't belong to us. 14But ask the Lord Jesus Christ to help you live as you should and don't make plans to enjoy evil.

For further thought

1. Compare Rom. 13:1,2 with Ezra 7:26; Eccl. 8:2; Matt. 17:27; 22:21; Titus 3:1; I Peter 2:13. Why is the government to be obeyed? Could men live together without some form of government? Why?

2. What are your views on Rom. 13:1-7, in regard to revolution and fleeing from countries ruled by tyrants?

Is Paul suggesting in Rom. 13:1-7 that injustice is right? Compare Deut. 16:20; Ps. 82:3; Prov. 21:3; 29:27. Also see Acts 5:17-42, especially v. 29. Do you think that Christians who have fled communist countries did the right thing? What if you lived behind the Iron or Bamboo Curtain and had a chance to get out? Write down what you would do and why.

3. Memorize Rom. 13:10 in *Living Letters* paraphrase. To whom (in your family, school, place of work) do you owe "back payments" on your debt of love? (See Rom. 13:8.) Write down some specific plans for bringing that debt up to date soon.

CHAPTER 12

The game Christians play too well

"He's okay, but ... Well, I suppose the new plans make some sense, but ... I know I shouldn't judge, but any girl who would ... I suppose I shouldn't say anything; however, I feel it my duty to report that . . . Well, they're certainly entitled to their opinion, but it's difficult to see how they can get an idea like *that* out of the Bible ..."

Sound familiar? These are quotations from a well known game called "Evaluation." Other common pseudonyms for it are "Chop, Chop," "Judging Others," and "Sanctified Slander." In its most venomous form, it can turn into plain old gossip. It's a marvelous game. Simple to learn, and a perennial favorite. Any number can play and we usually all do to some extent. It's a game Christians play too well, as Paul points out ...

¹Give a warm welcome to any brother who wants to join you as a member of the church, even if he scarce believes that Christ alone can save him.

Don't criticize him for having different ideas from yours about what is right and wrong. ²For instance, don't argue with him about whether or not to eat meat that has been offered to idols. You may believe there is no harm in this, but the faith of others is weaker; they think it is wrong, and will go without any meat at all and eat vegetables rather than eat that kind of meat. ³Those who think it is all right to eat such meat must not look down on those who won't. And if you are one of those who won't, don't find fault with those who do. For God has accepted them to be His children. ⁴They are God's servants, not yours. Let Him tell them what to do. They are responsible to God, not you, and God will help them do what is right.

⁵Some think that Christians should observe the Jewish holidays as special days to worship God, but others say it is wrong and foolish to go to all that trouble for every day alike belongs to God. On questions of this kind everyone must decide for himself. ⁶If you have special days for worshiping the Lord, you are trying to honor Him; you are doing a good thing. So is the person who eats meat that has been offered to idols; he is thankful to the Lord for it; he is doing right. And the person who won't touch such meat, he too is anxious to please the Lord, and is thankful.

⁷We are not our own bosses to live or die as we ourselves might choose. ⁸Living or dying we follow the Lord. Living or dying we are His. ⁹That is why Christ died and rose again, so that He can be our Lord both while we live and when we die.

¹⁰You have no right to criticize your brother or look

down on him. Remember, each of us will stand personally before the Judgment Seat of Christ. [11]For it is written, "As I live," says the Lord, "every knee shall bow to me and every tongue confess to God." [12]Yes, each of us will give an account of himself to God.

Taboo or not taboo?

There's no doubt about it. The Christians in Rome were a diversified lot. They had a wide variety of backgrounds, from heathen paganism to Judaism. And, they were surrounded by countless pagan customs and practices. They constantly faced questions on what should a Christian do about this? Or that?

Paul didn't try to "help" these early Christians out of their dilemma by sending them a detailed list of do's and don'ts. Instead he gave them basic principles to guide Christian conduct and ethics.

For example, Paul deals in his letter with a problem that sounds strange today, but it certainly was very real for Roman Christians. It seems that some believers had their own set of "pure food" laws and they strictly abstained from eating meat of any kind. These vegetarians looked askance at Christians who enjoyed steaks and roasts without a twinge of conscience. In other cases, it was the *kind* of meat that might be called to question. Christians converted out of Jewry were scandalized by the idea of eating pork, for example. In addition there was an even more sticky question: "Was it right for a Christian to buy, serve or eat meat cut from animals used in pagan sacrifices?" This "pagan meat" was sold every day at a good price after pagan rituals were completed. It was good meat, too, as far as quality and taste were concerned. Only the best animals were used for sacrificial purposes.

Some Christians had no qualms about buying and eating the meat that was cut from animals offered to idols. To them idols were nothing more than carved pieces of wood or stone. The meat was unharmed, unchanged, and perfectly good to eat. But other Christians were horrified by the idea. To them the meat that came from animals used at pagan rituals was "spiritually contaminated," a part of heathendom and certainly not fit for a true Christian's menu.

"To eat meat or not to eat meat" was no small question in the church at Rome. Some "anti-meat Christians" even doubted the salvation of their "less scrupulous" brothers in Christ. (Now the story is beginning to sound more familiar.)

There were other problems—such as what day to worship on (vs. 5,6). Some Christians thought they should use the already established religious holidays for worshiping God. Other sincere believers pointed out that all days were for worshiping God, so why designate certain days as more important?

So it went, and so it still goes. The disagreements are different, but the results are the same. We Christians don't see eye to eye, and so we judge one another. We evaluate, we criticize, we tear down ... all in a very spiritual way of course. It is sort of a game, one version of which might be called, "Helping Others to Be Spiritual." Sample:

"Stop me if I'm wrong, George, but haven't you —uh, been spending a lot of money on a car?"

"Nope."

"No? You don't think the money could be better used, say in the leprosy fund?"*

Paul's advice on this kind of fun and games is brief. Don't do it. His logic is simple: You should not criticize another man's servant. Christians are all God's servants. Therefore ... (v. 4).

Now, this is good advice, but a question remains. How do you apply this rule to specific situations? Are you supposed to be so agreeable that you become a regular "good ole wishy-washy Charlie Brown"?

It helps if you understand what Paul is driving at in this passage. He is not saying that Christians can hold poles-apart views on basic doctrines like sin, the deity of Christ or salvation by faith. Paul is talking about disputable questions, that is, questions where two points of view are certainly valid and useful. To Paul the dispute over meat and holy days at Rome fell into this legitimately disputable category. And instead of ruling on who was right, Paul introduced a basic principle: There are many areas in life where the answer is not cut and dried or black or white. *The Christian must search his own conscience to see how he really feels—and what he really believes.* "On questions of this kind everyone must decide for himself" (v. 5).

Another key point is the identity of the "weaker

---

*From *Games Christians Play* by Judi Culbertson and Patti Bard. Copyright 1967. Harper and Row, Publishers.

brother" Paul mentions in v. 1. Some Christians tend to call another believer "weak" if he violates their particular set of taboos. Is this what Paul meant by "weak"? In chapter 14 he makes it quite clear that his sympathies in the dispute on meat are with those who feel free to eat it, whether it was offered in a pagan sacrifice or not. Paul is saying that those who live in freedom and liberty to violate the legalistic taboos of men are not the weak ones. *The legalists are weak* and need to be accepted and understood.

There are two lessons here:

1. It is easy to blow up a marginal question until it is completely out of proportion (as many a church has learned to its misery). Majoring in minors is almost always the road to destruction.

2. It is easy to judge the other fellow and call him "weak" or "shallow" because he has a personal habit or idea that you don't agree with, but in reality *you* may be the weaker one because you are living legalistically (religiously) instead of in Christian freedom and liberty.

Paul may not lay down a list of "do's and don'ts" on disputable issues, but he is quite specific about the basic reason why Christians should stop nursing their pet taboos and start loving and accepting one another as brothers in Christ. "We are not our own bosses to live or die as we ourselves might choose" (v. 7). The moment you begin criticizing someone else, you run the risk of slipping into the same sin that Adam committed: deciding you will become like God. But the Christian knows he is not final authority. "Living or dying we follow the Lord. Living or dying we are His" (v. 8).

Here is the key. It's our relationship with Christ that helps us understand why we shouldn't judge others. Who is first in the Christian's life? *Who is boss?* It is only as a Christian learns to let Christ be boss that he is able to live by His command to ". . . love one another, as I have loved you" (John 15:12).

And how do you show that you love the other fellow when you disagree with him? Actually, disagreements are key opportunities to practice Christian love. Christ was always willing to talk over a man's ideas with him. Here are some basic rules that the Lord taught and practiced. If you try them they can help you learn how to communicate with other people, instead of continuing to play judging games.

1. *Be Genuine.* In other words, be honest and open with other people. Be for real. Try dropping— a little at a time—your front, that vital piece of equipment for all Christian gamesmanship: the spiritual mask. The spiritual mask often has remarks like these coming from behind it:

"Yes, Lord willing, I hope to . . ."

"I just couldn't do that and take Jesus with me . . ."

"Before I do anything about this, I'll have to bathe the matter in prayer . . ."

And, of course, all masks aren't spiritual. There is the "dripping with honey" (but it's really venom) mask; the "I've got confidence in *me*" mask; the

BE GENUINE

TRY DROPPING THAT VITAL PIECE OF EQUIPMENT FOR CHRISTIAN GAMESMANSHIP, THE SPIRITUAL MASK . . .

"I've got *no* confidence in poor ole me" mask; and the well known "reverse English" mask: "One thing about me—I'm *honest*."

How do you gain the nerve to start peeling away, layer by layer, the particular mask that you operate behind? The answer lies in your relationship to Christ—your real (unmasked) relationship. As you build, bit by bit, this relationship on sincere faith that openly seeks God's will, the mask or masks you need for "social security" become less essential. Instead of having a spirit of fear, you learn to be . . . wise and strong, to love (people) and enjoy being with them. (See II Tim. 1:7, *Living Letters*.)

This way you can be genuine and at the same time the Spirit of Christ is at work in you, helping you to be sensitive and appropriate in your honesty and openness.

Appropriateness and sensitivity are vital to being genuine. Genuineness is not foolhardy frankness or asinine honesty. This is how judging and criticism and fighting often start. (After all, you only told the *truth* . . .) To paraphrase the old cliche, "Honesty

125

that is guided and empowered by the Holy Spirit is the best policy." Or, as the Lord put it: "It is the man who shares my life and whose life I share who proves fruitful" (John 15:5, *Phillips Translation*).

2. *Be Acceptant.* People talk a lot about "accepting one another." What do they mean? Is it really so simple as saying, "I accept him, you understand, but I *can't stand* his attitude" (or his taste in clothes, or his friends, or his personal habits).

All of us are self-conscious. Our image of self is directly related to how we feel, what we do, the things we like. Criticize a person's viewpoint, taste, or ideas and you criticize *him*, no matter how much you may mean otherwise.

Before turning your guns (especially your spiritual guns) on someone's ideas, actions or attitudes, ask yourself a couple of questions: Am I trying to help this person, or am I really trying to impose my value system on him? Do I respect and like this person for what he is, or am I trying to make him over to suit my idea of what is respectable, likeable or spiritual?

BE ACCEPTANT

DO I RESPECT AND LIKE PEOPLE FOR WHAT THEY ARE, OR DO I WANT TO MAKE THEM OVER— TO SUIT MY VALUES?

Does being acceptant sound difficult? It is. But it helps the Christian to remember that God has accepted him—just as he is. And the One who said, "Come unto me . . ." is also the One who said, "Stop judging superficially; you must judge fairly" (John 7:24, *Williams Translation*).

3. *Be Understanding*. Acceptance doesn't mean much unless it is matched by understanding. What is understanding? Whatever it is, it is not "knowing something" about someone, having him all figured out or being able to predict what he will do. This kind of "understanding" says: "I understand what is *wrong* with you." This isn't real understanding; it is evaluation (the same Christian game that is the subject of this chapter).

Perhaps one fellow best described understanding when he stated on a questionnaire that if someone wanted to understand him he ". . . should put himself in my shoes—I mean *really* put himself there."

This kind of understanding—putting yourself in the other fellow's shoes—is called empathy. When you show someone empathy, you mentally try to project your own conscious thoughts and ideas into the other person's being. That is, you try to see exactly how things seem to him.

You communicate empathy to other people more by your actions and facial expressions than you do by pat statements. For example, suppose someone disagrees with you on interpretation of a certain doctrine or verse in the Bible, or perhaps the disagreement is over something as simple as who will speak at the next get-together for your group. You can approach this disagreement in one of two basic

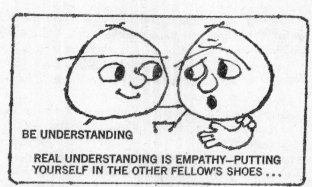

BE UNDERSTANDING

REAL UNDERSTANDING IS EMPATHY—PUTTING YOURSELF IN THE OTHER FELLOW'S SHOES ...

ways. You can say by word, action or with as little as a slight curl of your lip: "You're all wet, Buster. Why don't you go hide and forget to come out?" Or you can try empathy and sincerely say: "You don't like that idea? Well, I think I see your point. Let's try to work out something else ..."

The above is not a magic formula. Some people are so biased, so fearful, so unacceptant, that they wouldn't know empathy if it shouted in their ear. But the point is that as you seek to acquire an attitude of understanding toward others, there is much more chance that you will experience less disagreement, do less judging, less criticizing. At least you have nothing to lose, except some of your pride, fear and defensiveness, and those other "cherished characteristics" that make us more religious than Christian.

Be genuine. Be acceptant. Be understanding. These three simple rules were practiced and lived by the same Person who will one day judge us all. The best cure for criticism and judging others is to "Remember, (that) each of us will stand personally before the Judgment Seat of Christ . . . each of us will give an account of himself to God" (Rom. 14:10, 12).

For further thought

1. Memorize Rom. 14:10. From Rom. 14:1-12 list several other reasons why judging others is wrong.

2. Read Rom. 14:7-9. Paul is talking about Christians in these verses. Compare II Cor. 5:14-21; Gal. 2:20; Phil. 1:20,21. In a sentence write what the Lordship of Christ means to you.

3. Review the cartoons on pp. 125, 126, 128. Which of the tips on how to be less judgmental seem most useful to you? Being more genuine? Being more acceptant of others? Being more understanding (empathic) towards others? Why?

4. Do you think the following statement is true or false? "People often judge one another because of pride, fear or defensiveness." Write reasons for your answer.

CHAPTER 13

Stepping Stone? or Stumbling Block?

Stepping stone? Stumbling block? What kind of religious jargon is this? Well, it isn't jargon really. The term stumbling block is a good solid biblical word and it is also in Webster's, defined as "any cause of stumbling, perplexity, or error; any obstacle or impediment to steady progress." Paul has a few words on this idea of being an impediment to progress—specifically the progress of Christian growth in others. His solution is to become a "stepping stone"—that is, to be willing to be walked on for the sake and love of Christ. Is Paul carrying this Christian love idea past the Second Mile? See for yourself ...

¹³So don't criticize each other any more. Try instead to live in such a way that you will never make your brother stumble by letting him see you doing something he thinks is wrong. ¹⁴As a matter of fact, I am perfectly sure on the authority of the Lord Jesus that there is nothing really wrong with eating meat that has been offered to idols. But if someone feels it is wrong, then he shouldn't do it for it is wrong for him. ¹⁵If your brother is bothered by what you eat, you are not acting in love if you go ahead and eat it. Don't let your eating ruin someone for whom Christ died.

¹⁶Don't do that which will cause criticism against yourself even though you know that what you do is right. ¹⁷For after all the important thing for us as Christians is not what we eat or drink but stirring up goodness and peace and joy from the Holy Spirit. ¹⁸If you follow Christ's example in these affairs, God will be glad; and so will your friends. ¹⁹So aim for harmony in the church and to build each other up. ²⁰Don't undo the work of God for a chunk of meat. Remember, there is nothing wrong with the meat but it is wrong to eat it if it makes another stumble. ²¹The right thing to do is to quit eating meat or drinking wine or doing anything else that offends your brother or makes him sin by causing resentment or influencing him to do what he feels is wrong.

²²You may know that there is nothing wrong with what you plan, even from God's point of view, but keep it to yourself; don't flaunt your faith in front of others who might be hurt by it. In this situation, happy is the man who does not sin by doing what he knows is right.

²³But anyone who feels it is wrong shouldn't do it. He sins if he does, for he thinks it is wrong; and so for

him it is wrong. Anything that's done apart from what he feels is right is sin.

Romans 15:1-6

1-2Even if we believe that it makes no difference to the Lord that we do these things, still we cannot just go ahead and do them to please ourselves; for we must bear the "burden" of being considerate of the doubts and fears of others—of those who feel these things are wrong. Let's please the other fellow, not ourselves, if it is for his good and builds him up in the Lord.

3Christ didn't please Himself. As the prophets said, He came for the very purpose of suffering under the insults of those who were against the Lord.

4And these things that were written by God so long ago are to teach us patience and to encourage us, so that we will look expectantly to God for help.

5May God Who gives patience, steadiness, and encouragement help you to live in full harmony with each other—each with the attitude of Christ toward the other. 6And then all of us can praise the Lord together with one voice, giving glory to God, the Father of our Lord Jesus Christ.

It is not what you know that counts

In the first half of chapter 14 (to v. 12), Paul teaches that we should not criticize or judge others, especially fellow Christians. In debatable matters each Christian is free to do whatever he feels is right, according to his own conscience. No Christian is to judge other Christians, because God will be the final judge of all (vs. 10 and 12).

Yes, Paul does teach this—in Rom. 14:1-12. But now, lest his readers become too intoxicated with the heady wine of liberty, Paul turns the coin over and introduces a sobering thought. *Freedom to follow convictions must be balanced by personal responsibility to do what is best for your brother in Christ.*

The question is not, "Can I feel free to do this or that?" The question becomes, "How can I fulfill my responsibility to help others live and grow in the Christian life?"

The Christian is to live in such a way that he does not cause his brother to stumble, and this includes the pesky dispute concerning meat eaters vs. vegetarians that Paul handled in Rom. 14:1-12.* Paul, who really sided with the meat eaters, now turns around and says that even though a man is free to eat meat if his conscience allows him to, that same man should not live in disregard for the man whose conscience would be offended by a practice like eating meat. (See v. 14.) Paul did not want to misuse his freedom of conscience in any way that might tempt or influence someone to do something he felt was wrong, something that damaged his feelings of fellowship and rapport with Christ.

How do you apply this principle today? Christians do not disagree over eating meat, especially the kind of meat offered to idols. But Christians do disagree over a multitude of practices: from mixed bathing to types of dress and cosmetics; from what is proper behavior on Sunday to what is proper entertainment; from what beverages a person may drink to what kind of job he may hold. And what is

---

*If you want to review this controversy, see pp. 120, 121.

right in one part of the country is wrong in another. What is acceptable to one group is not acceptable to another, often in the same church. There is no universal outlook and no universal specific solution to these problems. There is, however, a universal principle to apply to them all: the principle that Paul has been discussing for the last several chapters—love.

In v. 15 Paul makes it clear: "If your brother is bothered by what you eat, you are not acting in love if you go ahead and eat it. Don't let your eating ruin someone for whom Christ died."

... *Ruin someone for whom Christ died.* That's a different matter. When you look at it that way, the issue is no longer simply a disagreement between two sides or two points of view. Paul is actually saying that even though your viewpoint may be perfectly valid, you still may have to "lose the battle" in order to win the war against evil as you fight for the good of others in the body of Christ.

In these latter chapters of Romans (12-15), Paul emphasizes in various ways the challenge in Christian service: to glorify God, not yourself. In order to glorify God, the Christian often must choose between satisfying his own preferences in favor of serving Christ. As Paul says, "Don't undo the work of God for a chunk of meat" (or for the sake of enjoying a certain pastime on Sunday afternoon, for the sake of looking "chic" in a certain style, for the sake of a favored form of entertainment). There may be nothing wrong with the meat (or its equivalent), but it is wrong to do anything that may cause a Christian brother to stumble, be

134

TRYING TO REGULATE YOUR LIFE TO PLEASE
EVERY CHRISTIAN'S IDEA OF "TABOO OR NOT TABOO"
WOULD BE A GOOD WAY TO GO INSANE...

confused—led away from, instead of closer to
Christ.

Paul sums it up in v. 21: "The right thing to do is
to quit eating meat or drinking wine or doing
anything else that offends your brother or makes
him sin by causing resentment or influencing him
to do what he feels is wrong."

Paul is saying that in many cases *what you know*
is not the point; at the heart of the matter is *how
you love* and how you help build others in the faith.

"All very good," you may say, "but is this kind
of thing really so relevant for me—today? Nobody I
know jumps me about the things I do. I must be
exempt from this stumbling block business, or am I
supposed to throw away my razor because there are
Christians who don't believe in shaving?"

Don't excuse yourself on either count. For one
thing, trying to regulate your life to please every

Christian's idea of "taboo or not taboo" would be a great way to go insane. At best it would be the religiously laden path back to legalism, which is precisely what Paul is writing against in his letter to Rome. But what Paul is suggesting is that every Christian should be ready and willing to do what appears necessary to help another Christian within his sphere of influence.

Secondly, Paul is really not as concerned about "not being a stumbling block" as he is about "becoming a stepping stone."

In so many words, then, Paul is saying that to not be a stumbling block is good, but to seek to be a stepping stone is even better. To be a stepping stone means that you are actively in search of ways to help others draw closer to Christ. (Remember the "debt of love" in chapter 13? You never finish paying *that*.) Being a stepping stone implies that you will be walked on. The idea of being walked on doesn't seem too appealing or glamorous, but then neither is getting crucified on the town garbage dump while cynics talk smut and soldiers curse and gamble for your clothes.

All right, let's say the principle is plain enough, but still you're left wondering: "Just *how* do I go about being a stepping stone, not a stumbling block? How can I even find out who is stumbling over me? Do I go around church and take an opinion poll on my TV habits? Do I get up in prayer meeting and confess that I sneaked out of town to see 'Sound of Music'?"

Much more useful would be to, first, review the ideas on being genuine, acceptant and understanding of others (pp. 124-128). In addition you might try working on being a *listener*—not at keyholes or on phone taps, but just in casual everyday conversations. In a word, *really listen* when people talk to you.

Listening has become a lost art. Lack of real listening is at the roots of the poor communication that is prevalent at all levels and in all areas today. Employees and employers don't really listen to one another. Teachers and students do not listen to each other and neither do parents and children. Everyone seems to have his transmitter on (to give his own opinion), but few of us seem willing to give our receiver a chance to really hear what the other fellow is trying to tell us.

For example, when did you last commit the error illustrated in the cartoon on page 139? Yesterday? This morning? Ten minutes ago? The situation is usually quite simple: Two people are talking. One is trying to explain his point of view, how he feels. Is the other person really listening to him? Not on your hearing aid! This other guy is too busy thinking about what he's going to say in return. A lot of exchanges between people are not conversations; they are competitions, and may the loudest, most clever, or most stubborn transmitter win.

Exactly what does listening have to do with being a stepping stone? For one thing, perhaps people are sending you signals on your behavior, but you're not hearing them because you aren't trying. People do a lot of communicating indirectly, non-verbally. To get the full message from people, you often have to listen to *how* they are saying something, as well as the words themselves. Perhaps you have friends who really *are* bothered by some of your habits or attitudes, but they would prefer to die before they would openly come out and admit it. Instead they drop an occasional offhand remark, or perhaps they don't say anything, but their facial expression tells the story. (Many of us not only fail to listen to others; we don't really see them either. Have you ever watched two people talking and each is treating the other like a post? They look past one another, at the floor, at the ceiling, at the object they are working on or discussing, *but seldom at each other*.)

In order to be a good listener (and looker), you need an attitude of empathy and understanding. (See pp. 127, 128.) You *must want to hear* the other person before you will be willing to really listen to him. Listening is a practical, and much needed way of being a stepping stone. (Some people aren't the easiest folk to listen to under any circumstances.) People are used to being talked at (or about). But most of us are pleasantly surprised when someone is willing to talk *with us* and listen to what we are saying and feeling.

Try being a listener. Solomon was correct: "He that answereth a matter before he heareth it, it is folly and shame unto him ... A wise man will hear, and will increase learning" (Proverbs 18:13; 1:5).

Also, real listening is an excellent way to put I John 3:18 into action: ". . . let us stop just *saying* we love people; let us *really* love them, and *show it* by our actions" (*Living Letters*). To love is to have the attitude of Christ toward others (Rom. 15:5).

138

This kind of attitude is willing to go out of its way, suffer inconvenience, *be stepped on* in order to serve and help. Christ's kind of love has no motive but the good of others; it expects nothing in return, it only seeks to give.

Christian service is not mechanical attention to duty. It is not a "legal obligation." Christian service is not performed chiefly for the "good of the community." Christian service—being a stepping stone, not a stumbling block—has the highest possible motive: to glorify God. And when a Christian truly serves with this purpose, he invariably reaches out to those around him with concern and love because God is love.

J. B. Phillips' translation of Rom. 15:5-7 sums it up this way: "May the God who inspires men to endure, and gives them a Father's care, give you a mind united toward one another because of your common loyalty to Jesus Christ. And then, as one man, you will sing from the heart the praises of God the Father of our Lord Jesus Christ. So open your hearts to one another as Christ has opened his heart to you, and God will be glorified."

For further thought

1. Memorize Rom. 14:13. Then read Rom. 14:13-21. Then write your own definition of "stumbling block" and "stepping stone." Which is it easier to be? Why?

2. Try an experiment this week. Pick one or two people you don't usually listen to very closely and try to *really hear* what they are saying. Analyze *how* they say things and *why* they say things as well as *what* they say. See if this helps your relationship with these people. See if you learn anything about being a stepping stone instead of a stumbling block.

3. Compare Rom. 15:1-6 with these vs. on glorifying God: Ps. 22:23; Matt. 5:16; John 15:8; I Cor. 6:20. What do you feel is your best means of glorifying God? Write down some specific ideas.

CHAPTER 14

DIVIDE or MULTIPLY

One of the marks of the early Christians was love. Celsus, anti-Christian Roman philosopher of the second century, had to grudgingly admit: "Behold, how these Christians love one another." And today ... behold, how many Christians stay in their tight little cliques, talking much of loving, but not showing much unity in their living. Were the early Christians more spiritual than believers today? Did they possess some strange power that made them able to love one another constantly and consistently? Hardly. Loving one another didn't come any easier for the first Christians than it does for us. In fact, in some ways it was harder. In the closing lines of his letter Paul includes some tips on how to be united around Christ. They are tips any Christian can use ...

⁷So, warmly welcome each other into the church, just as Christ has warmly welcomed you; then God will be glorified.

⁸Remember that Jesus Christ came to help the Jews, so that He could fulfill the promises God made to their ancestors. ⁹And remember that the Gentiles give glory to God for His mercies to them. That is what the Psalmist meant when he wrote: "I shall praise You among the Gentiles, and sing to Your name." ¹⁰And in another place, "Be glad, O you Gentiles, along with His people the Jews." ¹¹And yet again, "Praise the Lord, O you Gentiles, let everyone praise Him." ¹²And the prophet Isaiah said, "There shall be an Heir in the house of Jesse, and He will be King over the Gentiles; they will pin their hopes on Him alone." ¹³So I pray for you Gentiles that God Who gives you hope will keep you happy and full of peace as you believe in Him. I pray that God will help you overflow with hope in Him through the Holy Spirit's power within you.

¹⁴I know that you are wise and good, my brothers, and that you know these things so well that you are able to teach others all about them. ¹⁵⁻¹⁶But even so I have been bold enough to emphasize some of these points, knowing that all you need is this reminder from me; for I am, by God's grace, a special messenger from Jesus Christ to you Gentiles bringing you the Gospel and offering you up as a fragrant sacrifice to God; for you have been made pure and pleasing to Him by the Holy Spirit.

¹⁷So it is right for me to be a little proud of all Christ Jesus has done for you through me. ¹⁸I dare not judge how effectively He has used others, but I know this: He has used me to win the Gentiles to God. ¹⁹I have won them by my message and by the good way I

have lived before them, and by miracles done through me as signs from God—all by the Holy Spirit's power. In this way I have preached the full Gospel of Christ all the way from Jerusalem clear over into Illyricum. 20But my ambition is to go and preach where the name of Christ has never yet been heard, rather than where a church has already been started by someone else. 21I want to follow the plan spoken of in the Scriptures where Isaiah says that those who have never heard the name of Christ before will see and understand.

22That is why I have been so long in coming to visit you. 23But now at last I am through with my work here, and I am ready to come after all these long years of waiting. 24So when I take the trip to Spain I am planning, I will stop off there in Rome; and after we have had a good time together for a little while, you can start me on my way again.

25First, though, I must go down to Jerusalem to carry a gift to the Christians there. 26For you see, the Christians in Macedonia and Achaia have taken up an offering for those in Jerusalem who are going through some hard times. 27They were very glad to do this, for they feel that they owe a real debt to the Jerusalem Christians. Why? Because the news about Christ came to them from the church in Jerusalem. And since they received this wonderful spiritual gift of the Gospel from them, they feel that the least they can do in return is to give them some food!

28As soon as I have delivered this money and completed this good deed of theirs, I will come to see you on my way to Spain. 29And I am sure that when I come the Lord will give me a great blessing for you.

30Will you be my prayer partners? For the Lord Jesus Christ's sake, and because of your love for me—given to you by the Holy Spirit—pray much with me for my work. [31]Pray that I will be protected from those who are not Christians in Jerusalem. Pray also that the Christians there will be willing to accept the money I am bringing them. [32]Then I will be able to come to you with a happy heart by the will of God, and we can refresh each other.

[33]And now may our God, Who gives peace, be with you all. Amen.

Do you deal in potential or the past?

At first glance these verses may appear to be sort of earthy, the tacked on final thoughts of a man who is hurrying to finish up what has been a rather long letter. There are, however, some practical principles for Christian unity in what Paul writes.

First, Paul had hope, even for the "hopeless" situations. In vs. 7-13 he touches once more on the "civil rights" problem of the early church: Jew vs. Gentile. Jewish believers felt they had an inside track with God. After all, they were descendants of Abraham, members of a race that God chose to glorify His name and preserve His Word. Many Jews became Christian converts in the first years of the church and they held no little resentment and disdain for the "intrusion" of the Gentiles who also believed in Christ and wanted to be in the Christian fellowship.

Some of the more zealous Jews tried to force Gentiles to go through "initiation ceremonies" like circumcision before they were allowed into the church. It was hard for the good Jew, steeped in tradition—law, religion—to accept the idea that the gospel offered free salvation to all men on the basis

THE EARLY CHURCH HAD ITS OWN CIVIL
RIGHTS PROBLEM. JEWISH CHRISTIANS LOOKED
DOWN ON GENTILES AS "OUTSIDERS."

of faith and faith alone. Many Jewish converts to Christianity did not completely accept or understand the concept of grace—God's unmerited love and favor. They preferred to keep Christianity in the religious category, garnished with requirements, rituals and rules.

The Gentiles, however, had little religious tradition and training. They came out of paganism, gladly accepting the idea that through Christ they could know forgiveness of sins and have salvation. They could not understand why the Jews made such a fuss, or why some Jewish believers seemed to look down on them because of their lack of religious training and background. There was a great deal of confusion, misunderstanding and friction because of this basic problem of Jew and Gentile in the same Christian congregation. This internal dispute was perhaps the greatest danger the Christian church faced in its early years, and Paul knew it. That is why he deliberately designed his letter to the Romans and another letter to the church in Galatia to deal with the problem and explain why and how Christians should unite around the concept of salvation by faith in Christ.

Paul faced heavy odds and personal abuse of every kind in order to draw Christians together around Christ. Still, he kept going. A key to his attitude is in Rom. 15:13. If Paul could pray that others would gain hope, peace and happiness from God, then he had experienced it himself. He experienced it *as he believed God.* He experienced hope and inner peace as he allowed the Holy Spirit's power to work in and through him—another example of the difference between being religious and being Christian.

And then, Paul had tact. You have to read between the lines a bit, but it is there. In v. 14 he comments that he knows he really doesn't have to tell the Roman believers these basic things about love and glorifying God in a united fellowship. Paul doesn't nag them, bawl them out, or drop sarcastic remarks. Paul prefers to "think positive" and look for the good in the situation. Paul was much more interested in *what a man could be than in what a man had been.*

Here is another key point. Think about it. Do you

DO YOU EVER CARRY A "SANCTIFIED GRUDGE"?

see other people in the process of becoming something better or do you see them as bound by their past—what they have (or haven't) done or said (especially to you)? To put it plainly, do you carry a sanctified grudge against others in your family, at your school or place of work? It is easy to stereotype others. You can place them in neat little pigeonholes like "sloppy," "talk too much," "dishonest," "undependable," "unfair," etc., etc. But this is the way of religion, the way of the rules, the way of ideas and attitudes that are set in sanctimonious cement.

Christianity, however, deals in *potential*, in what a person can *become*, not only what he *is*. This is the heart of the gospel. If God had dealt with us

147

strictly on the basis of our past, he would never have sent Christ to die for our sins. But God loved us. He saw us as persons of worth, of value, with potential. He forgave and He keeps on forgiving, always looking toward what we can become if we respond to the opportunity we have in Christ.

Paul showed love by meeting his responsibilities. Paul made his plans *around* his duties, not *on top of* them. He longed to go to Spain, to carve still more frontier trails for the Gospel (v. 24). He hoped to make Rome a jumping off place for his expansion of missionary activities to the west. But first, there was this rather routine but urgent matter of taking a gift of money to the Christians in Jerusalem (v. 25). This gift was not some kind of bonus or special prize that the Jerusalem believers had won in a drawing. The money was badly needed, for those who were down and out.

In a city like Jerusalem much of the available employment must have been connected with the Jewish temple and the needs of this huge structure. But the temple was controlled and run by the Sadducees, a sect of Jewish leaders who denied belief in the resurrection and who were sworn enemies of Christ and Christianity. It must have been a frequent occurrence for men in Jerusalem to lose their jobs because of becoming Christians.

Because of the Sadducees and other zealous Jews who hated Christianity, Paul faced real danger in going to Jerusalem. As far as "old time religion" Jews were concerned, Paul was Public Enemy No. 1. He was wanted everywhere, and above all in Jerusalem. The Jews had tried to kill Paul more than once (see Acts 14:5; 18:12), and now he was planning to go right into their main headquarters to deliver "CARE" packages!

Paul could have easily begged off. He could have sent someone else while he hurried on to "more important matters" at Rome or in Spain. But Paul not only preached Christian love and unity, he also practiced it. Paul's Lord had said, "Greater love hath no man than this, that a man lay down his life for his friends" (John 15:13). And because of his desire to help the poor in Jerusalem, Paul would eventually lay down his life.* Paul was a living, walking example of what it means to turn Christian words into Christian deeds.

Doesn't Christian unity, trust, mutual love and understanding really rest on this principle—deeds, not just words? If all Christians became persons of their word, what would happen?

Paul wasn't the only Christian who kept his word and labored hard and long for the unity of believers in the gospel. There were hundreds, thousands like him and a few of the names pop up at the very end of his letter to Rome. There may not seem to be much help here for facing the frustrations of the twentieth century technopolis, but there is an interesting thread in chapter 16. See if you can trace it . . .

Romans 16:1-23

1-2Phoebe, a dear Christian woman from the town of

---

*Paul never left Jerusalem a free man. The Jews tried to kill him; he was saved by Roman arrest, eventually transported to Rome under guard and was finally executed by order of Caesar.

Cenchrea, will be coming to see you soon. She has worked hard in the church there. Receive her as your sister in the Lord, giving her a warm Christian welcome. Help her in every way you can, for she has helped many in their needs, including me.

³Tell Priscilla and Aquila "hello". They have been my fellow workers in the affairs of Christ Jesus. ⁴In fact, they risked their lives for me; and I am not the only one who is thankful to them; so are all the Gentile churches.

⁵Please give my greetings to all those who meet to worship in their home. Greet my good friend Epaenetus. He was the very first person to become a Christian in Asia.

⁶Remember me to Mary, too, who has worked so hard to help us.

⁷Then there are Andronicus and Junias, my relatives who were in prison with me. They are respected by the apostles, and became Christians before I did. Please give them my greetings.

⁸Say "hello" to Amplias, whom I love as one of God's own children. ⁹And Urbanus, our fellow worker, and beloved Stachys. ¹⁰Then there is Apelles, a good man whom the Lord approves, greet him for me. And give my best regards to those working at the house of Aristobulus.

¹¹Remember me to Herodion my relative. Remember me to the Christian slaves over at Narcissus House. ¹²Say "hello" to Tryphena and Tryphosa, the Lord's workers; and to dear Persis, who has worked so hard for the Lord. ¹³Greet Rufus for me, whom the Lord picked out to be His very own; and also his dear mother who has been such a mother to me. ¹⁴And please give my greetings to Asyncritus, Phlegon, Hermes, Patrobas, Hermas, and the other brothers who are with them.

¹⁵Give my love to Philologus, Julia, Nereus and his

sister, and to Olympas, and all the Christians who are with them. [16]Shake hands warmly with each other. All the churches here send you their greetings.

[17]And now there is one more thing to say before I end this letter. Stay away from those who cause divisions and scandals, teaching things about Christ that are against what you have been taught. [18]Such teachers are not working for our Lord Jesus, but only want gain for themselves. They are good speakers and simple-minded people are often fooled by them. [19]But everyone knows that you stand loyal and true. This makes me happy indeed. I want you to remain always very clear about what is right, and to stay innocent of any wrong. [20]The God of peace will soon crush Satan under your feet. The blessings from our Lord Jesus Christ be upon you.

[21]Timothy my fellow-worker, and Lucius and Jason and Sosipater, my relatives, send you their good wishes. [22]I, Tertius, the one who is writing this letter for Paul, send my greetings too, as a Christian brother. [23]Gaius says to say "hello" to you for him. I am his guest, and the church meets here in his home. Erastus, the city treasurer, sends you his greetings and so does Quartus, a Christian brother.

How will your 'One Sentence Summary' read?

This chapter almost makes you feel like you've broken into someone's desk and rifled some of his personal papers. Paul is talking directly to friends now and behind many of his brief comments are dramas that were never written, heroics and sacrifices that were never recorded. Bible scholars have done a great deal of speculating on just who these people were, where they came from and what eventually happened to them. A most useful observation, however, is the one by William Barclay who comments that in these verses Paul characterizes many of these people in a single sentence. "He was a hard worker." "He was a good man." "They risked their lives for me." If your friends or family were asked to sum you up in one sentence, what would that one sentence be?

For further thought

1. Review the three principles for promoting Christian unity that are talked about in this chapter: 1. to have hope; 2. to have tact; 3. to meet your responsibilities (be a person of your word). Can you think of specific ways that you can apply these principles to your life? List at least one idea for each principle.

2. Think of someone you have "pigeonholed" as "undependable," "sloppy," "no personality," "moody," "grumpy," etc. Then write down ideas on what you could do to treat this person in a more positive way, so that you would see him or her as not bound by the past but with potential to change and grow in the future.

3. Memorize this sentence from Rom. 15:13, *Living Letters* paraphrase: "I pray that God will help you overflow with hope in Him through the Holy Spirit's power within you." Then do a study on what the Bible says about "hope" by summarizing John 3:3; Prov. 14:32; Col. 1:5; Titus 2:13; I Peter 1:3.

Conclusion

Never look back

Paul's "handbook" on how to be a Christian without being religious is about to close.

You may or may not agree with the *definitions* of "Christian" and "religious." But Romans emphasizes that there is a definite *difference*.

According to Webster, a religion is a system of faith and of worship . . .

And a Christian does have that.

According to Webster, a religion is the service and adoration of God expressed in forms of worship . . .

And a Christian certainly does this.

According to Webster, religion is devotion fidelity, conscientiousness, an awareness or conviction of the existence of a supreme being, which arouses reverence, love, gratitude, the will to obey and serve.

THE RELIGIOUS MAN FASHIONS A GOD HE CAN HANDLE . . . A SMALL REPLICA OF HIMSELF

A Christian has all this too, and one thing more. The Christian has power.

And it's not a power he generates from within himself. He knows that what the Bible claims is true: a man's heart is deceitful, a rubber check that keeps bouncing no matter how neatly he writes on it.

A Christian's power comes from God—Someone beyond himself. Religion creates a "someone," or a "something," tailored to size, not too big, of course. Religion produces a god that is easy enough to handle, compact enough to tuck in the dresser drawer between Sundays. But Christianity doesn't talk about a God like this.

Christianity talks about a God that you can't keep at arm's length by "reaching out for Him." Christianity claims that God reached us and did something for all mankind: *He removed our guilt.* Outside of death, guilt is perhaps man's greatest enemy. Guilt is the gnawing, corrosive acid that eats at a person from inside, the instinctive knowledge that you aren't all you would have the rest of the world believe, that you really aren't fit to stand before a righteous, holy God.

Search the tomes of the religions, the cults, the sects. None of them truly claims to have an answer for sin and guilt. Many groups explain guilt away quite neatly by refusing to admit it is there. You'll have to make up your own mind about that. You'll have to consider the evidence: the pages of history, especially recent history that records two World Wars and an atomic standoff that specializes in international games of cops and robbers, with live ammunition. Or turn to the pages of your local newspaper. Crime is not exactly going out of style. If you're still not convinced be honest and consult your own experience, your own score in the game of life.

It all leaves us with one real claim to fame. We are all capable of self delusion and deceit, of chicanery and cruelty far beyond the imagination.

Someone commits murder or suicide. Someone gets mixed up in dope, winds up in a shotgun wedding, or just plain doublecrosses a good friend. We are shocked. We never thought a person as fine as "so and so" would be capable of *that*. But we are all capable. We are all sinners, fallen short of the glory of God.

Christianity deals honestly with this basic problem of sin and guilt. Christianity says the living God entered history. The Bible's clear teaching is that God became human flesh. He died on the cross, not simply a misunderstood itinerant preacher who didn't get the breaks, but as a Supreme Sacrifice to pay the penalty for all sin. And that wasn't all. The Bible plainly states that Christ rose from the dead. His followers saw not a ghost, not a figment of imagination but a risen body that could be touched, that even ate food.

Either all this is truth (not "myth") or Christianity is the supreme hoax of history, and not even fit to be called a "great religion." But if Christianity is not more than a mere religion, then it is not worth the paper the New Testament is printed on.

And perhaps the strangest thing of all is that God has given all of us the freedom to treat Him as we please. God entered history, yes, but He hardly took us by force. A stable is not the usual setting for a coronation. A cross is not the usual spot for a farewell address.

And so, if you wish, you can keep Christianity in the religion category. You can refuse to believe any of its amazing claims. You can classify it with the quaint folklore of Greek mythology. You can relegate it to the escapism of the Buddhists and Hindus. You can be generous and say it is filled with the wisdom of Taoism or Confucius.

It doesn't matter how you want to disbelieve. The results are the same. You remain captain of your fate. You keep God cut down to a comfortable size, something you can handle, something that doesn't become inconvenient. Actually, you worship a replica of your own god—yourself. In effect you tell the true God, "I don't need any help." And you don't get any.

MANY A CHRISTIAN
LOOKS AT CHRISTIAN LIVING LIKE
A POLE VAULTER EYES THE 20-FOOT BARRIER . . .

157

But there's the other way to reduce Christianity to a religion ... from the inside. Instead of refusing the gospel, you accept it. You "get saved." You join the church. You worship every Sunday with the fellowship of the redeemed.

But despite your claim to faith in God's grace, you mix being a Christian with being religious. You couch it in warm spiritual tones, but you feel your relationship to God still depends on how well you follow the rules and regulations. In short, it's still a matter of how well you perform, how high you reach.

Many a Christian looks at Christian living like a pole vaulter eyes the "20-foot barrier." He works on his form. (That is, he gets his praying down pat; he learns the right cliches and how to quote the favorite proof texts at the right psychological moment.) He constantly tries to find the springiest pole he can. (That is, he is always looking for the new spiritual author, the new conference speaker, some new spiritual giant with whom he can identify and thereby somehow have some of his spirituality rub off on him.) And naturally, like any good vaulter, he practices diligently (showing up at all the meetings and services, making sure he looks and sounds as spiritual as the next guy). But inside he doesn't really feel that he can ever do 20 feet. He still equates Christianity with "being good" and he just doesn't feel he'll ever be good enough.

Well, in one sense this kind of Christian is right. He isn't "good enough" and he never will be as long as he goes at it that way. To go back to the pole vault comparison for a second, the bar is not just

20 feet up. It's 1000 feet high and all the poles are toothpicks. Being a Christian is not a matter of making all the right moves, earning Biblical Brownie points or spiritual merit badges.

Being a Christian is a matter of faith, personal faith and commitment to Jesus Christ.

Yes, you've *heard* that before. But have you really *thought* about it? Remember how Peter tried walking on the water (Matt. 14:29,30)? He did fine until he took his eyes off Christ, until he looked back and started getting nervous over the size of the waves. He started to sink, and he wound up crying, "Lord, save me!" This is a perfect illustration of the daily choices we make which result in being Christian or being religious. You can live by faith, in a personal commitment to Christ, or you can look back, forget about Him ... and sink.

Like most of life, it's not completely "either, or." Most of us never completely sink; but we don't ride the top of the waves all the time either. A lot of the time we seem to sort of wade through life—up to our knees, waist, or necks in circumstances, self will and frustration.

In other words, we Christians seem to be incurably religious, constantly tempted to tack on the religious flourish, live by the rules, add a bit of self effort that puts our personal touch on things.

But God doesn't need our personal touch. He wants *us* and leave the striving to Him.

One thing that helps is to remember that Christianity is not a state of perfection. In Romans, Paul tells you how to have victory over sin but he doesn't tell you how to be perfect. Paul knew that being a Christian is not a destination. A Christian has not "arrived." Christianity is a *walk*, a way of life, a process of maturity.

Go back and read the high point of Paul's letter to Rome: chapter 8. The Christian cannot be separated from the love of Christ. The Christian *can* have victory. The Christian life *does* work, *as you follow after the Holy Spirit.*

If you want a summary of what it means to be a Christian without being religious, memorize Rom. 8:5. "Those who let themselves be controlled by their lower natures live only to please themselves; but those who follow after the Holy Spirit find themselves doing those things that please God."

And as you do those things that please God, *you please yourself.*

It isn't always easy. It isn't automatic. The Christian life means growth and change. Growth and change are often painful, and not everyone grows at the same rate. But as the Christian grows he sheds his religious facades and kindergarten concepts of God. He takes on the attitude of hope and confidence that Paul shows in his closing lines of Romans.

The Christian is committed to an almighty God in faith and obedience. The Christian is in touch with Christ, through the Holy Spirit, who dwells in him. The Christian is on speaking terms with his Lord. He does not pray once a month, once a week or even once a day to a God that is a relative stranger.

You can always tell when two people really know each other—when they really communicate. There is a relaxed comfortable atmosphere. There is no stiffness, no stuffiness; yet there is respect, trust, love. The Christian who hopes to scrape off the religious scales seeks this kind of relationship as he relies on the power of the life giving Spirit, the power that is his through Christ Jesus, the power that has freed him from the vicious circle of sin and death. (See Rom. 8:2, *Living Letters*.)

The Christian may slip. He may fail. He may sometimes sink a bit, but always his goal is not merely trying to follow a religion. The Christian has hope and power and potential that come from beyond himself. The Christian is growing, changing, becoming all that God has in mind for him to be. The Christian continually learns to trust, listen to, and glorify the Living God.

And he never looks back ...

Romans 16:24-27

"Goodbye. May the grace of our Lord Jesus Christ be with you all. I commit you to God, Who is able to make you strong and steady in the Lord, just as the Gospel says, and just as I have told you. This is God's plan of salvation for you Gentiles, kept secret from the beginning of time. But now as the prophets foretold and as God commands, this message is being preached everywhere, so that people all around the world will have faith in Christ and obey Him. To God, Who alone is wise, be the glory forever through Jesus Christ our Lord. Amen."

Sincerely,

Paul